AnimalWays

Crocodiles

AnimalWays

Crocodiles

JUDITH JANGO-COHEN

BENCHMARK BOOKS

MARSHALL CAVENDISH
NEW YORK

With thanks to Frank J. Mazzotti,
University of Florida, department of Wildlife Ecology,
for his expert reading of this manuscript.

Benchmark Books
Marshall Cavendish Corporation
99 White Plains Road
Tarrytown, NY 10591-9001

Library of Congress Cataloging-in-Publication Data
Jango-Cohen, Judith
Crocodiles / by Judith Jango-Cohen.
p. cm. — (Animalways)
Includes bibliographical references (p.).
Summary: Describes the evolution, physical characteristics, behavior, habitat, and folklore
of crocodiles and examines various species and related crocodilians.
ISBN 0-7614-1136-4
1. Crocodiles—Juvenile literature. [1. Crocodiles.] I. Title. II. Animalways (Tarrytown, N.Y.)
QL666.C925 J36   2001   597.98—dc21   99-058363

Photo research by Candlepants, Inc.

Cover photo: *Animals Animals*, Gerard Lacz

The photographs in this book are used by permission and through the courtesy of: *Animals
Animals*: Micheal Dick, 2, 91; Deeble & Stone/OSF, 9, 11, 55, 56, 63, 74, 75; A. Brando,
16; Zig Leszczynski, 33, 41, 42, 46; Joe McDonald, 36 (top), 60, 61, 89; Henry Ausloos, 36
(lower right); Michael Fogden, 37 (top right), 50; Jim Tuten, 37 (lower), 65; Ken Cole, 45;
M. Pitts, 48; Frank Krahmer, 52; Ted Levin, 69; Bruce Davidson, 72 (left), 84, back cover;
Austin J.Stevens, 72 (right); S. Osolinski, 78; Maresa Pryor, 81, 93; John Pontier, 88. *Photo
Researchers, Inc.*: Joyce Photographics, 12; Tom McHugh, 13, 36 (middle), 36 (lower left),
98; H. Reinhard/ OKAPIA, 15; Tim Davis, 20; NASA Science Photo Library, 30; Francois
Gohier, 32, 59; Simon D. Pollard, 37 (top left); Malcolm Boulton, 58; Nigel J. Dennis, 68;
Jeffrey W. Lang, 73, 94; Karl H. Switak, 76; Mary M. Thacher, 79; Michael James, 86;
Norm Thomas, 100. *Art Resource/Erich Lessing*: 18. Dr. Arthur Busbey of the Geology
Department at Texas Christian University: 23, 26, 27.

Printed in Italy

6 5 4 3 2 1

Contents

HERE ARE SOME OF THE MAIN PHYLA, CLASSES, AND ORDERS, WITH PHOTOGRAPHS OF
A TYPICAL ANIMAL FROM EACH GROUP.

Animal Kingdom

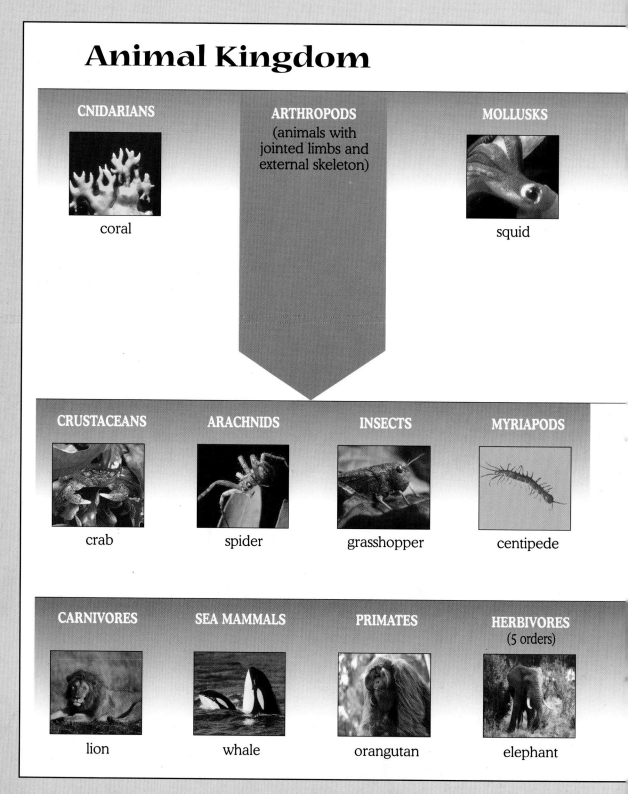

CNIDARIANS

coral

ARTHROPODS
(animals with
jointed limbs and
external skeleton)

MOLLUSKS

squid

CRUSTACEANS

crab

ARACHNIDS

spider

INSECTS

grasshopper

MYRIAPODS

centipede

CARNIVORES

lion

SEA MAMMALS

whale

PRIMATES

orangutan

HERBIVORES
(5 orders)

elephant

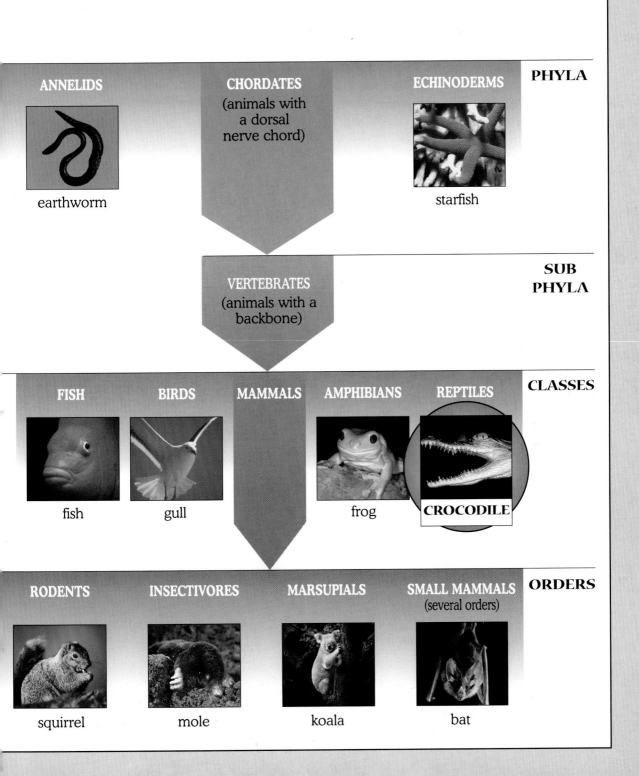

PHYLA

ANNELIDS

earthworm

CHORDATES
(animals with
a dorsal
nerve chord)

ECHINODERMS

starfish

**SUB
PHYLA**

VERTEBRATES
(animals with a
backbone)

CLASSES

FISH

fish

BIRDS

gull

MAMMALS

AMPHIBIANS

frog

REPTILES

CROCODILE

ORDERS

RODENTS

squirrel

INSECTIVORES

mole

MARSUPIALS

koala

SMALL MAMMALS
(several orders)

bat

1 The World of Crocodiles

There has been little rain, and the river has shriveled to pools dotting the sand. A young Nile crocodile lies on the back of a fat hippopotamus. It is safer there than in the water with the larger crocs. One of the pools churns as the big crocodiles feast on an antelope that has come down to drink. Gripping the antelope in their jaws, the reptiles spin furiously, ripping off chunks of flesh. Baboons sit and watch from the sand. Too wary to drink from the pool, they dig pits and sip from the water that seeps through.

Weeks later, the wet season rains have yet to come. Herons pick through the drying pool with their long bills, dining on stranded fish. Most herons are too quick for the crocodiles. But crocodiles pester them, knowing that startled herons may drop their catch. Antelopes and baboons, lounging in the heat, scramble to their feet and scurry away. A lion approaches. She is nursing cubs and needs to drink. Sniffing a water pit, she finds

FEEDING FRENZY. A TANGLE OF TAILS AND JAWS IS ALL THAT IS VISIBLE AS NILE CROCODILES FEED IN TANZANIA'S SERENGETI NATIONAL PARK.

that it is overtaken by bees, so she heads for the pool. While lapping up water, she eyes a line of watchful crocodiles. They make a low, rumbling roar, and the lion retreats to find a less risky drink.

Nine months have passed, but the usual rains have not fallen. Baboons guarding their water pits must fight off thirsty antelope and warthogs. The hippos have left. Even the crocodiles have abandoned the pool. Some have dug dens in the riverbank. But one crocodile, the largest and most dominant, remains. It lies alone, submerged in the mud. Six weeks later the pool has baked dry. Birds, baboons, and hippos have vanished. But deep in cool dens, crocodiles rest and watch and wait for the rains.

Life on the Edge

Crocodiles live on the edge—where mud and sand meet river and lake. Living on the border of land and water is critical to a crocodile's survival. In this habitat, crocodiles find an abundance of prey. Water provides foods such as fish, birds, and turtles. Water also draws land animals, such as antelope, that come down to the shore to drink. Crocodiles cannot chase an antelope as a lion can, but they do have an effective way of catching prey. Lying hidden in the shallow water, they leap up in a surprise attack. This hunting technique requires less energy than racing after prey. When food is scarce, being able to live on a low energy budget is an advantage.

In addition to providing good hunting grounds, a waterfront site is important for breeding. Crocodiles mate in the water and lay their eggs on land. Some crocodiles bury their eggs in holes they dig in the sand. Others, especially those that breed in the rainy season, nestle their eggs in tall mounds made of mud and plants. Once the hatchlings are born, however, they need the safety of shallow, plant-filled water. Babies still face many

THE EDGES OF LAKES AND RIVERS ARE CROCODILES' FAVORITE SPOTS. THEY CAN COOL OFF WHILE WATCHING FOR ANIMALS WHO COME TO DRINK.

predators, but they can find hiding places and food more easily here than on land.

Besides feeding and breeding, there is another reason this habitat is necessary for crocodiles. They need to be near both land and water to control their body temperature. Crocodiles are cold-blooded. Scientists use the term poikilothermic (*poikilo*, meaning various, and *therme*, meaning heat) because a crocodile's body temperature varies. Crocodiles are not like humans and other warm-blooded animals, who maintain a constant temperature. The human body works like a thermostat, which is set at about 98.6 degrees Fahrenheit (37˚C). If we begin to get overheated, our body reacts by sweating, to cool us down. If we are exposed to the cold, our bodies shiver, which warms us up.

To help hold in heat, most warm-blooded creatures are covered with fur or feathers.

A crocodile does not have this internal thermostat. Its body temperature goes up and down each day, by as much as 30 degrees. When basking in the sun, a crocodile's body temperature rises. If it rises too high, a crocodile heads to the water. Just dipping the tip of its tail in may be enough to cool it down. During the cool night, however, the water may be warmer than the air. This is because water loses heat more slowly than air. In this case, the crocodile will soak in the pool to stay warm.

Besides lacking their own thermostat, croccodiles differ from warm-blooded animals in another way. They do not have an internal heater. They cannot make body heat from the breakdown of food as warm-blooded creatures can. All the heat for their bodies must come from outside. That is why scientists

LOUNGING AROUND IS SERIOUS BUSINESS FOR CROCODILES. BY BASKING IN THE SUN, THIS JOHNSON'S CROCODILE RAISES ITS BODY TEMPERATURE SO IT CAN PERFORM ITS DAILY ACTIVITIES.

also describe crocodiles as ectothermic. (*Ecto* means external.) Being ectothermic gives the crocodile a big advantage. Unlike a warm-blooded animal, it does not need to feed an internal, food guzzling furnace. For this reason, crocodiles can get by with very little food.

Wherever land and water meet is a good spot for cold-blooded crocs—as long as it is hot. All fourteen crocodile species are found only in tropical and subtropical waterways. They do not live with penguins or polar bears. Unlike these warm-blooded creatures, their bodies cannot cope with the cold. Crocodiles have made their homes in all kinds of warm, aquatic habitats. Some species prefer freshwater rivers, lakes, and marshes. Others are found in saltier waters such as estuaries. There is even one species, the Indo-Pacific crocodile, that ventures out to sea.

THE INDO-PACIFIC CROCODILE LIVES IN SALTWATER HABITATS SUCH AS ESTUARIES. ALTHOUGH REMOVING THE EXCESS SALT FROM ITS BODY TAKES A LOT OF ENERGY, IT IS ABLE TO CATCH ENOUGH FOOD TO SURVIVE.

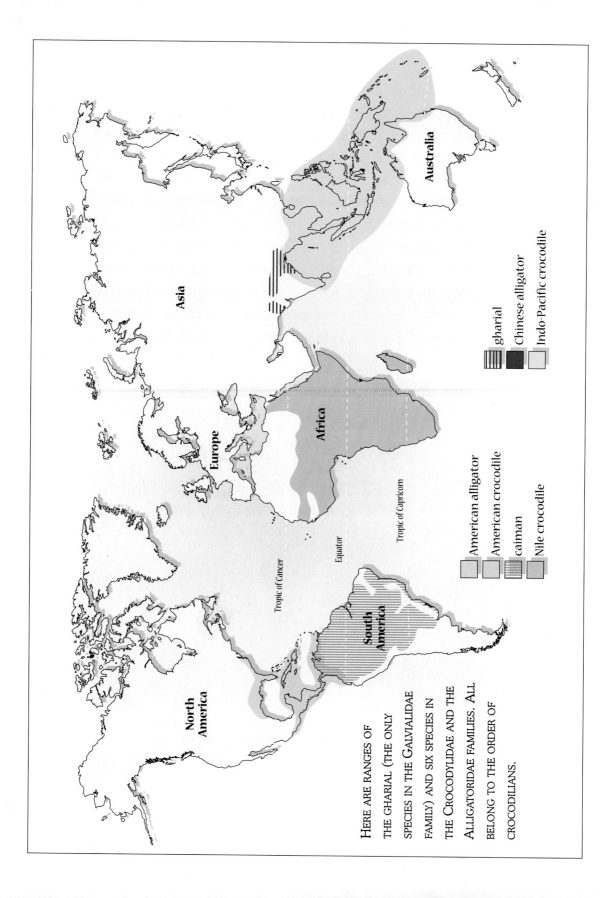

HERE ARE RANGES OF
THE GHARIAL (THE ONLY
SPECIES IN THE GALVIALIDAE
FAMILY) AND SIX SPECIES IN
THE CROCODYLIDAE AND THE
ALLIGATORIDAE FAMILIES. ALL
BELONG TO THE ORDER OF
CROCODILIANS.

North
America

South
America

Europe

Africa

Asia

Australia

Tropic of Cancer

Equator

Tropic of Capricorn

American alligator
American crocodile
caiman
Nile crocodile

gharial
Chinese alligator
Indo-Pacific crocodile

Besides choosing different types of wetland areas, the fourteen species of crocodiles differ physically. Crocodiles come in black, gray, green, brown, or tan, with yellow or black spots or bands. Snouts also vary, from broad and heavy to narrow. Crocodiles range from the giant 23-foot (7-m) Indo-Pacific crocodile to the African dwarf crocodile, which grows to only about 6.5 feet (2 m) long.

These physical variations also result in differences in behavior. Small- or narrow-snouted species, such as the dwarf and the African slender-snouted crocodiles, feed on crabs, fish, and frogs. Large- or broad-snouted species, such as the Indo-Pacific and the Nile, can tackle pigs and waterbirds. As their size

THE LONG, SLENDER SNOUT OF THE JOHNSON'S CROCODILE SWEEPS EASILY THROUGH THE WATER IN SEARCH OF FISH. ITS NARROW JAWS CAN ALSO PROBE BURROWS FOR CRABS.

THESE YOUNG REPTILES ARE NOT CROCODILES. THEY ARE RELATIVES CALLED
CAIMANS. LIKE CROCODILES, CAIMAN SPECIES VARY IN SIZE, RANGING FROM 5 TO 20
FEET (1.5 TO 6M).

increases, so does the proportion of their diet that includes
mammals. The largest crocs can bring down wildebeest, horses,
and even leopards.

Both Nile and Indo-Pacific crocodiles will also attack people. This is due to their tremendous size and because both
species live in waterways near people. In developed regions,
where people use crocodile habitat for recreation, stories about
clashes with crocodiles abound. One such story involves an
Australian safari guide who was attacked by an Indo-Pacific
crocodile while trying to free his grounded airboat. Although he
was badly mauled, he managed to survive because his female
partner held onto him from the bank.

In less developed areas, people regularly fish, bathe, wash

clothes, and drive cattle in waterways inhabited by crocodiles. For thousands of years, the crocodile has been a perilous element in their lives. It is no wonder that crocodile myths and legends are an intricate part of these cultures. Even today, people carry charms for safety and recite spells to ward off an attack.

Ancient Egypt

The ancient Egyptians lived alongside the crocodile. Although they relied upon a supply of spells for protection, they also recited prayers to the crocodile asking for protection. This may seem odd, but although the Egyptians feared this predator, they also respected its ferocity and strength. To summon the crocodile's power, they made wands from the curved tusks of the hippopotamus. They carved imaginary clawed beasts and crocodiles with jagged teeth into the ivory. Anxious Egyptian parents held these wands and whispered spells as they kissed their infants at night. They begged the beasts to keep their sleeping children safe from scorpions and snakes.

The great respect that Egyptians held for crocodiles was often reported in stories by visitors to their land. One observer to the ancient city of Crocodilopolis told of being in a splendid temple garden. Egyptian priests entered the garden carrying a large tray that held cake, roasted meat, and wine sweetened with honey. Near a pool, basking on the sun-warmed sand, lay a magnificent crocodile. Gold ornaments glistened in its ears, and bracelets adorned its front paws. Two priests approached the beast and opened its jaws. Another priest fed the reptile a meal of cake and meat and poured the honeyed wine down its throat.

The crocodile was sacred here. Residents believed that the fertility god, Sobek, especially loved the crocodile. Why did they connect fertility with the crocodile? In September, when the

Nile River flooded, it brought mineral-rich silt, which fertilized the fields. It also brought the crocodiles. Because of this Egyptians felt that Sobek favored this reptile and released his spirit into the crocodile when appearing on Earth.

To honor Sobek, Egyptians built ornate temples. Artists decorated the walls with images of crocodiles. Sculptors carved towering statues depicting Sobek with a human body and a crocodile head. At each temple, priests selected one crocodile to be kept and honored. Later, sanctuaries were built where many crocodiles were raised and bred. When these crocodiles died,

A PHARAOH MAKES AN OFFERING TO THE ANCIENT EGYPTIAN CROCODILE GOD SOBEK. THIS RELIEF WAS CARVED ON THE TEMPLE OF SOBEK AND HORUS, WHERE PILGRIMS CAME TO REGAIN THEIR HEALTH.

undertakers bathed their bodies in a special salt, called natron, to dry out the tissues. Then they wrapped the crocodiles in papyrus leaves and perfumed cloth. These preserved bodies were placed in decorated coffins and buried in special cemeteries.

After a while, a tremendous business developed around these crocodile mummies. Crocodiles kept in sanctuaries were often killed when young, usually by having their necks wrung. Their bodies were mummified and worshipers visiting the temple would buy them. Because these people believed that a crocodile had an afterlife, they hoped the crocodile would bring their requests to Sobek. Later, priests gathered the mummies, which were left at the temple, and placed them in underground tombs. Thousands of these mummies have been unearthed by archaeologists.

Magic, Myth, and Medicine

Ancient people in other parts of the world had their own beliefs about crocodiles, many of which centered around their teeth. In some areas of Africa, tribal people equipped themselves with crocodile-tooth necklaces. They believed that these charms provided protection from crocodile attacks. The charm was considered especially powerful if it came from a crocodile that had eaten a villager. The people of Peru, in South America, also wore crocodile teeth. Here though, the teeth were not worn as a protection against attack, but to prevent poisoning. In Asia, witch doctors used crocodile teeth as a death charm. To prepare the charm, they filled the hollow tooth with herbs. Then they painted it red, and coated it with fat from the body of a human corpse. When the tooth was prepared, they made a bow from a flexible young tree. As they fired off the tooth, they entreated it to find and pierce the intended victim's heart.

Other parts of the crocodile's body were also believed to

EACH TOOTH IN THIS INDO-PACIFIC CROCODILE'S MOUTH WILL EVENTUALLY FALL OUT AND BE REPLACED. IN ITS LIFETIME, A CROCODILE MAY SPROUT MORE THAN FORTY SETS OF TEETH.

hold powers. Egyptian physicians prescribed a mixture of crocodile fat and dung to cure river blindness. This disease is actually caused by a parasitic roundworm, but Egyptians believed that it was caused by the crocodile. As the physician applied the crocodile concoction he chanted, "The crocodile is now weak and powerless." Elsewhere in the world, doctors used charred crocodile skin and vinegar as a painkiller. Children with whooping cough were fed crocodile meat. Even as late as 1880, Americans with tuberculosis were advised to swallow crocodile oil. There is no evidence that any of these treatments were effective.

A common belief among people throughout the world was that humans were descendants of the crocodile. In certain areas of New Guinea, people tell a version of this story about a crocodile ancestor who is also the Creator:

> *Before mountains stood, before there were canyons, deserts, and woods, there was water. The water was still and empty. No fish swam. No crabs crawled. No weeds floated upon its waves. Then Crocodile called out and land ascended from the sea. The new earth split open, and Crocodile, father of all, planted his seed. The land came alive. Vines and grasses grew. Snakes slithered and birds flew. Humans drew their first breaths. Next Crocodile gave his great lower jaw to the earth and turned his upper jaw into the sky. Then the sun rose upon the first day.*

In Madagascar, an island off the east coast of Africa, there is a clan called Son of Crocodile. When a member of the clan dies, one of the elders hammers a long nail into the corpse's forehead. The nail is removed at burial, freeing the body to join its crocodile ancestors. The clan believes that within the grave the corpse turns into a crocodile and goes to live with its relatives in the river. Villagers in Africa also used to believe that the spirits of the dead dwelled in crocodiles. Boys would leave food for these spirits, hoping that in return, the spirits would protect their village. In many parts of the world, gifts such as the body organs of dead kings, the bodies of enemies, and even live human sacrifices have been offered to crocodile relatives.

2 Past and Present

Poking out from behind a clump of ferns is a skinny tail. Attached to the tail is a small, scaly body perched on long, slender legs. Short claws line its four quick feet. The creature does not move. Its eyes are fixed on the top of a tree stump. A skittish lizard pokes its head out of the stump and then scurries down the trunk. *Snap!* The lizard is scooped up by sharp teeth in powerful jaws. This skinny, long-legged predator was not a crocodile. However, many scientists believe that these reptiles, called sphenosuchians, are the crocodile's closest ancestors.

THE HISTORY OF CROCODILES BEGINS ABOUT 200 MILLION YEARS AGO. This was when the dinosaurs first appeared, as well as those wide-winged reptiles, the pterosaurs. Crocodiles, dinosaurs, and pterosaurs all belonged to a group of reptiles called archosaurs (*arch*, meaning chief, and *saur*, meaning lizard). Archosaurs weren't lizards, but they were the chief or "ruling reptiles" for 140 million years during the Mesozoic era. (*Homo sapiens*, or the

---

*ORTHOSUCHUS.*THIS SOUTH AFRICAN PROTOSUCHIAN IS AMONG THE MOST ANCIENT CROCODILES IN THE WORLD— ABOUT 200 MILLION YEARS OLD. IT WAS LESS THAN 3 FEET (1 M) LONG AND LOOKED LIKE A LIZARD, WITH ITS LONG LEGS AND SHORT SNOUT.

human species, have been around for less than one million years.)

Scientists can tell that these three groups were related by looking at clues from their bones. One feature they all had in common was their hind limbs were longer than their forelimbs. Another is they all had two large skull openings behind each eye socket and another hole in front of their eyes. The holes in these skulls actually made them stronger and better able to withstand the rigors of biting. (They are similar to the openings between the crisscrossing struts of a bridge.) They lighten the skull and give the muscles more places to attach, making for more powerful jaws.

In these powerful jaws were a new kind of teeth. For 200 million years all teeth had sat on top of the bone. They were connected only by small bands of fibers. (Sharks still have this type of tooth.) But these archosaurs had teeth that were anchored in deep sockets within the bone, so they did not fall out as easily. For this reason, archosaurs are also called thecodontians, meaning socket-toothed.

First Forms—Protosuchians

What were the first crocodiles like? Did they glide through the seas or run about on land? Did they have claws or hooves on their feet? Were they giants like *Tyrannosaurus* or as small as a dog? Did they eat meat or plants? The answer? All of the above. Ancient crocodiles came in many varieties. They evolved into different forms as time went on, but there was always an interesting assortment living at once.

Scientists divide crocodile evolution into three main stages. The earliest crocodiles are called protosuchians (*proto*, meaning first or earliest form). They were about 3 feet (1 m) long from head to trailing tail. Protosuchians moved easily on land with four long legs. Two rows of hard plates protected their backs and tails, and a bony shield covered their bellies. These first crocodiles appeared about 215 million years ago in the late Triassic. At this time all the continents were clumped together into one supercontinent called Pangaea. Because protosuchians could travel from continent to continent, their fossils have been found in what is now North and South America, southern Africa, Europe, and eastern Asia.

The Middle Crocodiles—Mesosuchians

The early Jurassic period saw the emergence of the mesosuchians (*meso*, meaning middle). Some of these crocodiles were land based, or terrestrial, predators like the protosuchians, but these later forms were much bigger. One group was called sebecids, after Sobek, the crocodile-god from ancient Egypt. When the dinosaurs disappeared, they became the most fearsome terrestrial predator on the continent of South America. That is, until large meat-eating mammals arrived. The competition from these carnivores may have led to the sebecids' extinction.

While terrestrial crocodiles dominated the land, marine mesosuchians patrolled the oceans. *Teleosaurus* was a sleek, armored crocodile. Its long, slender snout was lined with pointed teeth, that were perfect for grabbing seafood such as fish and squid. When swimming, *Teleosaurus* may have held its short limbs by its side, as modern crocodiles do. Some mesosuchians were so well adapted to ocean life that their limbs were shaped like paddles. *Metriorhynchus* was a marine crocodile with flippers and a tail fin at the tip of its 10-foot (3-m) body. Fossils of *Metriorhynchus* show that it ate monstrous fish six times its size. One fossil's stomach also contained what look like the bones of a pterosaur. This flying reptile may have been snagged while

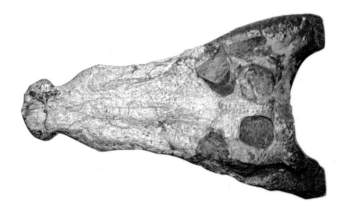

skimming the water for fish. Fossils have not been found to tell us how *Metriorhynchus* reproduced. It probably moved too awkwardly on land to lay eggs like modern crocodiles. It may have given birth to live young as some sea snakes do today.

Another group of mesosuchians spent time both on land and in water. One of these amphibious crocodiles was *Bernissartia*. It reached a maximum length of just 3 feet (1 m) and had several long rows of armor covering its back. The front of its mouth was equipped with sharp teeth that were ideal for catching fish. Broad, flat teeth in the back of the jaws may have been used to crush shellfish or perhaps to eat dead animals found on land. Not all amphibious crocodiles were small, though. One mesosuchian called *Sarcosuchus* was eleven times longer than *Bernissartia*. Its skull alone was the length of two of the smaller crocodiles. Fossils of this huge species have been found in both South America and Africa.

Another mesosuchian crocodile found in China had scientists confused for thirty years. They named the strange beast *Chimaerasuchus paradoxus*. (A chimera is an unreal creature. A paradox is a contradiction.) What was so weird about this crocodile? It ate only plants. How could scientists tell it was a herbivore? Its teeth were rather flat with a cutting edge at the back—perfect for clipping and chewing plant fibers. So while other crocodiles dined on dinosaurs, *Chimaerasuchus* happily fed on ferns.

Cretaceous Crocodiles—Eusuchians

The most advanced group of crocodiles first appeared in the late Cretaceous, about 80 million years ago. These are the eusuchians, the group to which modern crocodiles belong. One of the early eusuchians, *Deinosuchus*, (terrible crocodile) was so tremendous that when scientists first found its bones, they thought it was a dinosaur. At 50 feet long (15m) it was the size of *Tyrannosaurus*. Like *Tyrannosaurus*, it probably preyed on herbivorous dinosaurs that lived in ponds and marshes in what is now the United States. Other eusuchians were entirely terrestrial, such as *Pristichampus*, a sharp-toothed crocodile with no claws. It did have hooves, though. *Pristichampus* may have been a predator, or perhaps a scavenger, feeding on dead animals. Members of this group were still living in Australia no more than 2 million years ago.

As crocodiles were evolving from protosuchians to mesosuchians to eusuchians, they were steadily heading in two main directions. Over millions of years their spines were becoming stronger and more flexible. This happened as the bones of the spine, the vertebrae, gradually changed shape. Crocodiles

DIPLOCYNODON. THIS 50-MILLION-YEAR-OLD EUSUCHIAN FOSSIL WAS UNEARTHED FROM SWAMP DEPOSITS IN GERMANY. IT LIVED THROUGHOUT EUROPE UNTIL THE PLEISTOCENE ICE AGE AND IS A RELATIVE OF MODERN CROCODILES AND CAIMANS.

Crocodile Evolution

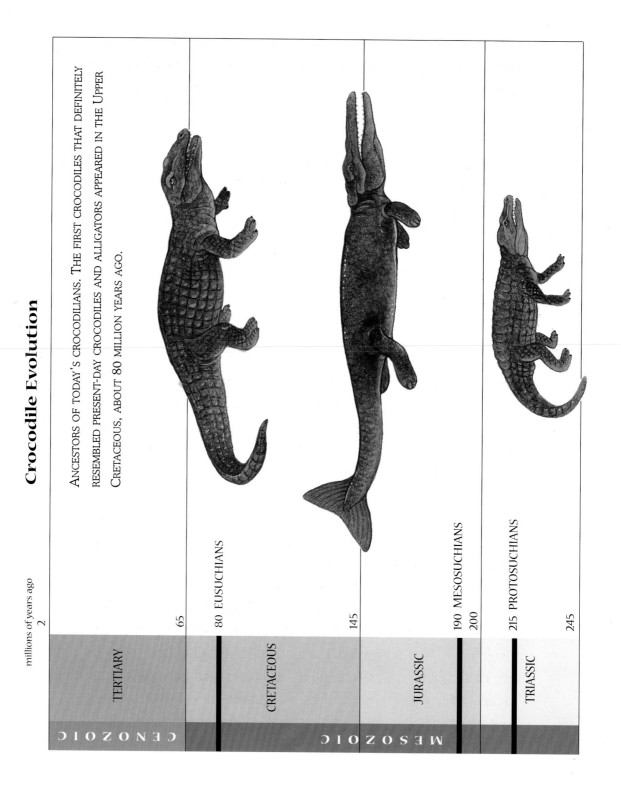

Ancestors of today's crocodilians. The first crocodiles that definitely resembled present-day crocodiles and alligators appeared in the Upper Cretaceous, about 80 million years ago.

millions of years ago

2

65

80 EUSUCHIANS

145

190 MESOSUCHIANS

200

215 PROTOSUCHIANS

245

TERTIARY

CRETACEOUS

JURASSIC

TRIASSIC

CENOZOIC

MESOZOIC

were also evolving in another important way. Their throats were changing so that their mouths could be sealed off from their breathing passages. This development helped crocodiles because when water got into their mouths, it would not flow into their lungs.

These early eusuchians survived so successfully, that 80 million years later, their descendants still populate the earth. During their long journey through time, crocodiles have met many challenges—from competing creatures and from drastic changes on the earth. Sixty-five million years ago the earth experienced such a devastating change that scientists are not certain how crocodiles survived.

Survival

Imagine an asteroid with a diameter of 6 miles (10 km) crashing to Earth. The explosion it causes is equal to one million erupting volcanoes. Glowing missiles of rock ignite fires that incinerate about one quarter of the world's plants. For months, cinders and soot choke out the sun. Bullets of burning acid rain blast the cold, dark earth.

Many scientists believe that such a collision occurred 65 million years ago at the close of the Mesozoic era. How do they know, since humans were not around to witness it? The rocks tell stories. An element that is rarely found on Earth, called iridium, has been found in 65-million-year-old rocks all over the world. Although iridium is scarce on Earth, it is commonly found in meteorites. Shocked quartz and melted glassy spheres, which are evidence of an impact, have also been found in the iridium layer. Other evidence includes a 113-mile-wide (80-km) crater that was formed 65 million years ago off the coast of Mexico.

Some scientists speculate that the result of this impact was

AN ARTIST IMAGINES A GIGANTIC ASTEROID STRIKING THE EARTH. MANY SCIENTISTS BELIEVE THAT A SMALLER ASTEROID DID HIT THE EARTH 65 MILLION YEARS AGO. LAND CREATURES SUCH AS DINOSAURS BECAME EXTINCT, WHILE THOSE UNDERWATER, SUCH AS CROCODILES, SURVIVED.

the death of the dinosaurs. It may also have caused the extinction of about 70 percent of all other species. On land, many flowering plants perished, which meant death to a great number of herbivorous animals. Carnivores that ate these herbivores died as well. Tiny marine plants and animals, called plankton, also perished. Since plankton is the basis of the ocean's food web, marine life dwindled.

What survived? Some plants grew back from seeds and roots. Little mammals that could burrow into the ground also survived. In fact, mammals began to flourish once the dinosaurs disappeared. What about the crocodiles? Some scientists believe that they escaped extinction because some of them lived in freshwater habitats. The food webs in these habitats may not have been as disturbed. We do not know their secret, but somehow they lived on to enter the Cenozoic era.

At the beginning of this era, crocodiles lived throughout the world. Crocodile fossils have been found on every continent except Antarctica. But about 38 million years ago, many crocodile species began to go extinct. This extinction coincided with a cooling of the earth's climate. By the Pleistocene Ice Age, 2 million years ago, there were no longer any crocodiles in Europe. All the remaining species now lived in warmer areas, closer to the equator.

Besides the climate change, the growing number of mammals also affected the survival of various crocodile species. After the demise of the dinosaurs, large carnivorous mammals evolved and began to thrive. For the terrestrial crocodiles, such as the large sebecids and the hooved pristichampians, this meant competition, and eventually, extinction. But one terrestrial crocodile, whose fossils were discovered in 1980, actually survived until about 1,700 years ago. Living on the isolated island of New Caledonia, near Australia, this crocodile did not have many large mammals to compete with. It was probably hunted out of existence by the first human settlers.

Modern Crocodilians

Today there are no hooved, herbivorous, or finned crocodiles. The striking varieties found in ancient forms do not appear in their modern descendants. Overall, the members of the crocodile family are more similar than different. They all live in tropical or subtropical lowlands where they have adapted to an amphibious lifestyle. All are strong swimmers, propelled mainly by their

LIKE CROCODILES, COMMON CAIMANS ARE SKILLFUL SWIMMERS. DURING THE DRY SEASON, GROUPS CROWD THE REMAINING WATERWAYS.

powerful tails. And all crocodiles are carnivores that are very effective at hunting from the water.

The fourteen species in the crocodile family are part of a larger group of reptiles called crocodilians. The crocodilians are made up of three families: the crocodiles (Crocodylidae), the alligators and caimans (Alligatoridae), and the gharial (Gavialidae). The Alligatoridae family includes two species of alligator and six species of caiman. The Gavialidae family is made up of just one species, the gharial. All these crocodilians are very similar, so much so that some scientists classify them as members of the same family.

Scientists decide how to classify—sort and name living organisms—based on their body structure and on how closely they are related. As scientists gather more information about species, the classification of that organism may change. The system of classification we use today was developed in 1758 by a

A YOUNG COMMON CAIMAN HUNTS MOSTLY CRABS AND AQUATIC INSECTS. OLDER
CAIMANS PURSUE FISH AND EVEN WILD PIGS.

Swedish naturalist named Carolus Linnaeus. According to this
system, the largest group is the kingdom and the most basic unit
is the species. The American alligator would be classified in the
following sequence:

> Kingdom: Animalia (animals)
> Phylum: Chordata (spinal column)
> Class: Reptilia (reptiles)
> Order: Crocodylia (crocodilians)
> Family: Alligatoridae
> Genus: *Alligator*
> Species: *Alligator mississippiensis*

Fourteen of the twenty-three crocodilian species are in the
Crocodylidae family. This family is split into three genera, or related groups of species. The "true crocodiles" (genus *Crocodylus*)
contains twelve species. This genus includes such well-known

species as the American crocodile and the Nile crocodile. The genus *Osteolaemus* is represented by the dwarf crocodile. This crocodile from west and central Africa is the smallest of the crocodiles. The remaining species of crocodile is the false gharial (genus *Tomistoma*). Because of its slender snout it resembles the gharial. The false gharial's snout, however, is not as long. Some scientists classify the false gharialas part of the gharial family. Research on the relationship between these two species continues.

The Gavialidae family contains one species: *Gavialis gangeticus*. This crocodilian lives in the northern part of the Indian

Snout Comparisons

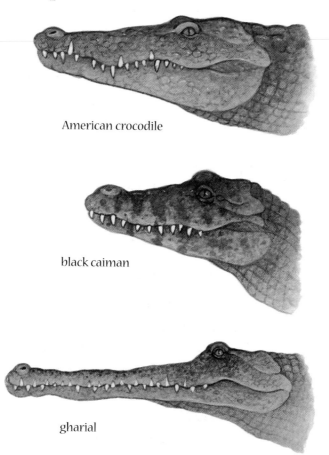

American crocodile

black caiman

gharial

subcontinent. Its long, slender snout is lined with interlocking teeth like a zipper. Of all the crocodilians, it is the most aquatic. Its legs are weak and do not allow it to move easily on land.

The Alligatoridae family is composed of two species of alligator and six species of caiman. Both alligator species live in warm temperate regions, unlike the crocodilians who reside in subtropical or tropical areas. The American alligator (*Alligator mississippiensis*) lives in the southeastern United States. The Chinese alligator (*Alligator sinensis*) is found in the lower Yangtze River area of China. The six remaining species of the alligator family include three species of caiman (genus *Caiman*), two species of dwarf caiman (genus *Paleosuchus*), and the black caiman (genus *Melanosuchus*). All six species of caiman live in the tropical rain forest wetlands of Central and South America. The caiman, like the alligator, can be distinguished from the crocodile because all of its lower teeth fit neatly into pits in its upper jaw. So when its mouth is closed, only its top teeth are visible. A crocodile's toothier bite shows lower teeth as well.

Family: Crocodylidae
    Genus: *Crocodylus*—12 species
    Genus: *Osteolaemus*—1 species
    Genus: *Tomistoma*—1 species

Family: Alligatoridae
    Genus: *Alligator*—2 species
    Genus: *Caiman*—3 species
    Genus: *Paleosuchus*—2 species
    Genus: *Melanosuchus*—1 species

Family: Gavialidae
    Genus: *Gavialis*—1 species

A LOOK AT CROCODILIANS FROM ALL THREE FAMILIES REVEALS DIFFERENCES AMONG SPECIES, AS WELL AS SIMILARITIES. EACH CROCODILIAN IS LABELED WITH ITS LATIN FAMILY NAME FOLLOWED BY ITS COMMON SPECIES NAME.

Crocodylidae: Nile crocodile

Crocodylidae: American crocodile

Crocodylidae: dwarf crocodile

Alligatoridae: American alligator

Crocodylidae: saltwater crocodile

Gavialidae: gharial

Crocodylidae: spectacled caiman

Extended Family

Taxonomists, scientists who classify organisms, have long wondered which living animals are most closely related to crocodilians. Is it the scaly-skinned lizards and snakes, the bony-backed turtles, or the feathered birds? Studying the skulls of these living creatures shows that lizards, snakes, and birds have two skull openings behind their eyes like the crocodiles. Turtles have none. Ancient skulls tell us more. Extinct forms of birds have a hole in front of their eye sockets like ancient crocodiles. Lizards and snakes do not. This fossil evidence points to birds as the closest crocodilian relatives.

A bird-crocodile connection may sound strange, but most scientists are convinced that birds evolved from that crocodile relative, the dinosaur. Evidence links birds with the therapod dinosaurs, who were meat eaters, had a long tail, and walked on two legs. They include the tremendous *Tyrannosaurus* and little *Compsognathus*, which is often compared to a chicken. Scientists even believe that some of these dinosaurs may have had feathers. Feathers would have provided insulation, attracted mates, and may have given added speed. Comparing today's birds and crocodiles reveals a lot of similarities. Both have scaly feet with claws, a four-chambered heart, and a muscular stomach for grinding food. Like birds, crocodiles lay eggs, build nests out of plants, and some care for their young.

Although fossils can help taxonomists determine how closely organisms are related, they cannot provide all the necessary information. Only the hard parts of organisms, such as bones and teeth, are usually preserved. Many other characteristics of the organism are lost, and are not available for study. Recently however, scientists have begun examining a different type of evidence to determine the crocodilians' closest relatives. They are looking at genes. Genes contain the code for making us who we

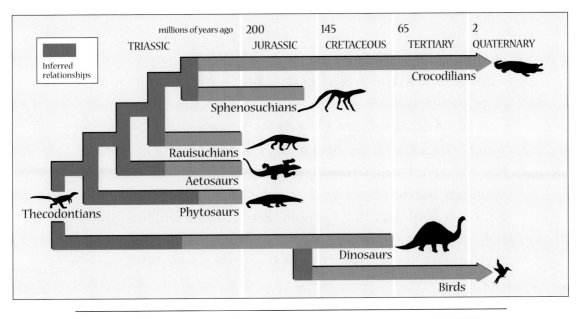

THIS SIMPLIFIED CHART SHOWS THE COMMON, IF DISTANT, CONNECTIONS AMONG CROCODILES, DINOSAURS, AND BIRDS.

are—a person, a crocodile, or a canary. The more closely two organisms are related, the more similar their genes. Some of these scientists studying genetic evidence found results that surprised them. Their findings indicated that turtles were the crocodile's closest relatives. But what about the missing holes in the skull? Some scientists studying fossilized turtle skulls believe that turtles started out with these holes and then lost them.

Is there any fossil evidence to support a turtle-crocodile connection? There were archosaurs called aetosaurs, which resembled present-day turtles with their small heads, beaklike jaws, and bony armor. They also had a shield, called a plastron, on their underside like turtles. Looking at today's creatures, turtles and crocodiles are the only backboned, four-footed animals that have horny plates on their backs and bellies. So who are the crocodilians' closest relatives? Are they the birds or the turtles? As long as scientists are curious, the detective work will continue.

3

Crocodile Construction

Crocodiles have been swimming, stalking, and eating for millions of years. During that time continents have broken apart, glaciers have advanced and retreated, and countless species have come and have gone. But through it all, the crocodile lives on. To what does this creature owe its success? The crocodile has been able to adapt to its environment. From its bony plated skin to its four-chambered heart, the crocodile's body is designed for survival.

Skin and Bones

One reason for the crocodile's successful survival is only skin deep. Imagine if all the skin on your body were protected by a layer of fingernail material. Crocodile skin is! The outer layer of a crocodile's scales is made of a protein called keratin. This is a tough coating that protects the crocodile. It is also watertight, which helps the crocodile keep in moisture. This keratin layer is

BUILT TO LAST. CROCODILES HAVE SURVIVED 200 MILLION YEARS OF CHANGE ON EARTH.

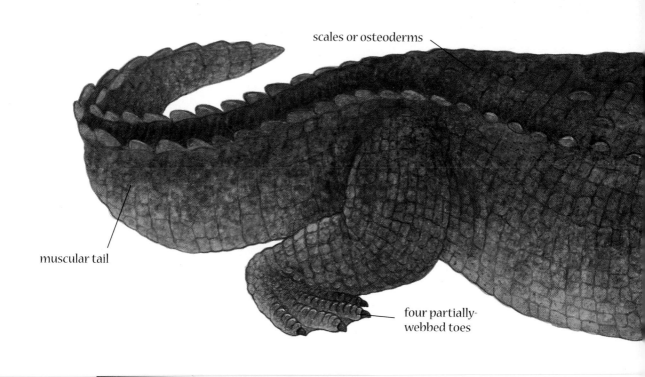

scales or osteoderms

muscular tail

four partially-
webbed toes

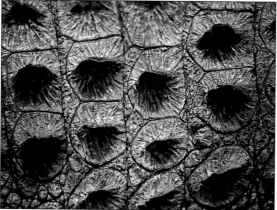

THE SKIN OF THE NILE
CROCODILE'S BACK IS
EMBEDDED WITH BONY
OSTEODERMS—AN
EFFECTIVE ARMOR. SOME
MEMBERS OF THE SPECIES
ALSO HAVE OSTEODERMS
ON THEIR BELLIES.

made of dead cells that don't grow with the crocodile. They must be shed. Since crocodile scales don't overlap, the covering of each scale is shed separately rather than altogether like a snake's.

For added protection, crocodiles have plates of bone embedded in their skin, called osteoderms (*osteo*, meaning bone, and *derm*, meaning skin). These bony projections lining a crocodile's back are interconnected, which allows for some

Crocodile Body

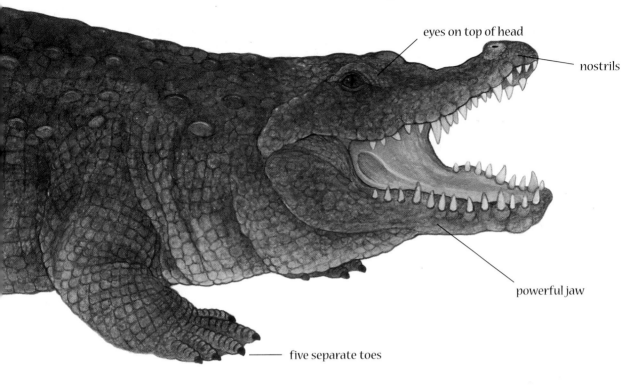

eyes on top of head

nostrils

powerful jaw

five separate toes

flexibility. They work like armor to shield the crocodile against attack and to safeguard its internal body organs. Some crocodiles even have osteoderms in their belly scales. The amount of bony protection varies among species. Large American crocodiles have fewer osteoderms on their backs than any other species. However, the dwarf crocodile has a heavily armored back and belly. This small species has traded greater protection for less flexibility.

Besides having a protective external skeleton, crocodiles, like all vertebrates, also have an internal skeleton. Their bony skull encases and protects the brain. There are two openings behind the eyes. Although it seems strange, these skull holes have allowed the crocodile to develop strong jaw muscles. When a crocodile closes its jaws, the muscles become shorter and wider. (This also happens to a rubber band when it springs back from being stretched.) Skull holes give a crocodile's jaw muscles room to expand. They may also provide additional places for the jaw muscles to attach to the bone. Crocodiles need powerful jaw muscles to capture prey.

As the crocodile skeleton evolved over millions of years, the vertebrae gradually changed shape. The early protosuchians had vertebrae that were spool shaped, much like a human's. The later eusuchians, however, evolved vertebrae that fit together like a ball and socket. This is the kind of joint people have in their hips and shoulders. Crocodiles use the added flexibility offered by the ball-and-socket vertebrae to crawl, walk, and swim. When they need to move quickly, they twist their trunk and tail in a fluid, s-shaped movement.

Because of the structure of a crocodile's ankle joint, crocodiles can move like no other reptile. They can walk. All reptiles can crawl or slide along the ground. In fact, "*reptilis*" is the Latin word for creeping. But a crocodile's ankle joint is built like a peg and socket. This allows its legs to rotate almost directly beneath its body. Raising their bellies off the ground, crocodiles can

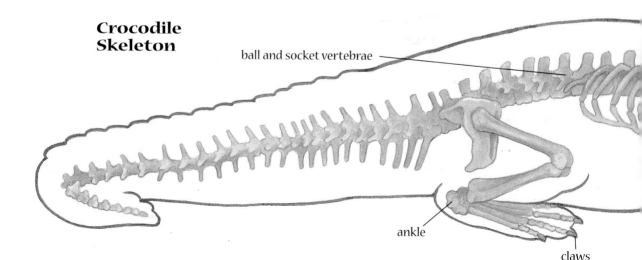

Crocodile Skeleton

ball and socket vertebrae

ankle

claws

CROCODILIANS ARE THE ONLY LIVING REPTILES THAT CAN RAISE THEMSELVES OFF THE GROUND TO WALK.

move in a dignified high walk. This high walk comes in handy for stepping over rocks and logs, and for moving over dry, rough ground. Crocodiles also use the high walk to climb steep riverbanks or to travel to a new water hole. As they walk, webbing on their feet keeps them from sinking into mud. Claws on their

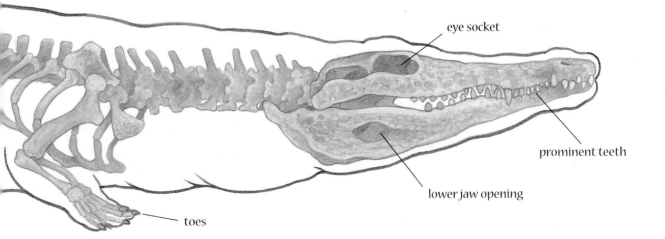

eye socket

prominent teeth

lower jaw opening

toes

WEBBING ON CROCODILES' FEET HELPS THEM PADDLE THROUGH THE WATER. AND JUST AS SNOWSHOES ALLOW PEOPLE TO DISTRIBUTE THEIR WEIGHT, WEBBING HELPS CROCODILES WALK MORE EASILY ON MUD.

toes grip the ground, and strong legs carry them far.

Crocodiles can also break into a fast high walk or a run to escape from danger. When moving quickly, though, they sometimes lose their balance and fall onto their chest and belly. Then, in typical reptilian style, they twist from side to side, gliding on the smooth scales on their bellies and tails. Like lizards, their legs help pull them along. Crocodiles use this belly crawl on mud or sand near the water. They can slip in quickly to escape danger or quietly to surprise prey.

Heart and Lungs

Being able to move in a high walk distinguishes crocodiles from other reptiles. But crocodiles differ from their fellow reptiles in another way. Other reptiles have a three-chambered heart. Crocodiles, like birds and mammals, have a heart with four chambers. Their heart, which pumps blood through their body, has two upper chambers, called the atria, that receive blood. It also has two lower chambers, called the ventricles, that release blood. The heart is also divided into a right and left side. Blood rich in oxygen from the lungs enters the left atrium and is released by the left ventricle to the body. Blood poor in oxygen enters the right atrium and is released by the right ventricle to the lungs. There it picks up more oxygen. With a four-chambered heart, the oxygenated blood does not mix with oxygen-poor blood. Other reptiles, with two atria and only one ventricle, do not have as efficient a system.

Besides pumping blood through the body, the heart also controls the flow of oxygen when a crocodile is underwater. To conserve oxygen, the heart slows down. Because the heart is not beating as fast, the body doesn't use as much oxygen. This increases the time that a crocodile can stay submerged because less oxygen is removed from the lungs.

A crocodile's lungs are similar to a turtle's but different from those of other reptiles. The lungs of crocodiles and turtles look like a sponge. Many large chambers are filled with a lot of small pockets for holding air. (Lizards and snakes have fewer of these air-trapping folds.) Underwater, crocodiles use this supply of stored air the same way a scuba diver uses an oxygen tank.

THIS CROCODILE IS ABLE TO FLOAT BECAUSE IT HAS STORED ENOUGH AIR IN ITS
LUNGS TO SUPPORT ITS WEIGHT.

Crocodile Organs

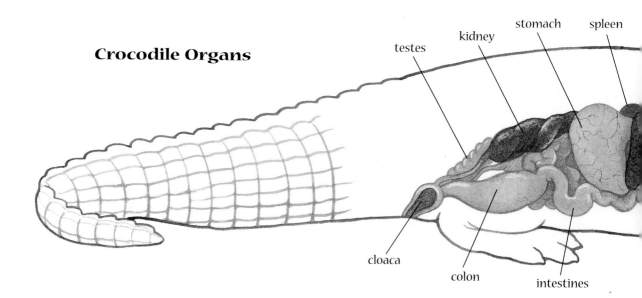

Normally, crocodiles stay underwater for no more than fifteen minutes during a dive. But when avoiding a threat, they can remain submerged for twice that long without taking a breath.

Eyes

Crocodile eyes are like the lenses of binoculars; they are set right next to each other. When a crocodile looks at an object, the field of vision from each eye overlaps. This binocular vision allows crocodiles to judge the distance of their prey with accuracy. To see how this works, close one eye at a time while reaching out to touch a distant object. It's much easier when both your eyes are open, isn't it?

Binoculars are not enough in the dark, though, and crocodiles often hunt at night. They can't carry a flashlight, but they do have a built-in reflector at the back of each eye. This reflective layer, called the tapetum, bounces light back to the eye's light-receiving cells. Getting a double dose of light increases the crocodile's night vision.

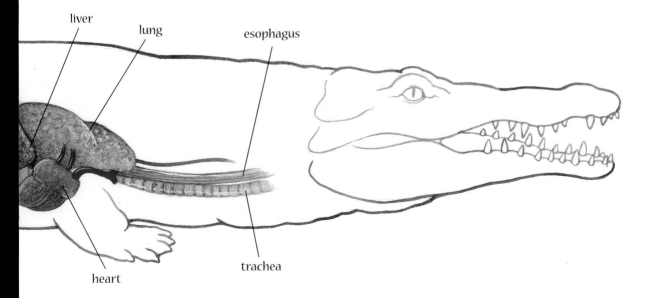

liver
lung
esophagus
heart
trachea

When light hits a crocodile's eyes, it enters an opening called the pupil. If a crocodile is hunting at dawn or at dusk the pupil opening is wide and round. This allows it to gather a lot of the scarce light. When the crocodile is lounging in the sun, its pupil looks like a long, thin slit. Under bright conditions, this slight opening lets in enough light. The human eye works the same way. The only difference is the human pupil closes to a small dot.

Crocodiles have an extra eyelid, too, called a nictitating membrane. The lids act like windshield wipers, sweeping dirt

THIS CROCODILE'S PUPILS WILL EXPAND IN THE DARK, GIVING IT NIGHT VISION EQUAL TO AN OWL'S.

across the eye and into the corner. When crocodiles dive, the membranes protect their eyes like a pair of goggles. Though the lids are transparent, the crocodile cannot focus through them underwater. When submerged, the reptile must use other senses, such as hearing. They can hear well both above and below the water. Their ears are right behind their eyes, covered by a long skin flap. When they dive, they close these flaps so that water does not leak in.

Teeth and Stomach

A crocodile jaw holds about sixty to seventy teeth. Most are shaped like cones with pointed tips, giving them a good grip. The rear teeth tend to be blunt. They can be used for crushing body parts like turtle shells and bones. Because of its teeth, a crocodile is supremely successful at gripping and crushing prey. But credit must also be given to its mighty jaws. Powerful muscles snap the jaws shut with crushing force and keep them clamped down on struggling prey.

With all this clamping, tearing, and crushing, crocodiles continuously wear out and lose teeth. Unlike humans, their teeth are not rooted in their jaws. Each tooth fits into a socket, from which it may fall out. Underneath, though, another tooth is growing. It begins to develop in a side pocket of the tooth socket. Eventually it moves into place under the old tooth, where it continues to grow. Meanwhile, tissue holding the old tooth in its socket begins to break down. When the old tooth is shed, the new tooth is ready to replace it.

Crocodiles swallow huge chunks of meat without chewing. Their teeth are simply not designed for chewing or cutting. Crocodiles are equipped with a mouthful of forks and no knives. Therefore, when tackling large prey, they must use the grip, roll,

THE DIFFERENT SIZES OF TEETH IN THIS CROCODILE'S JAW ARE THE RESULT OF NEW TEETH GROWING IN AT VARIOUS STAGES.

and rip method of eating. First they pierce their prey with their pronglike teeth. Then they roll around in the water until a chunk rips off. This piece may still be too big to swallow. If so, they hold it in their jaws while shaking their heads to thrash the meat against the water.

The food that a crocodile swallows enters a three-chambered

stomach. The main chamber is the thick-walled fundus. Here, strong muscles mix the food. In addition, stones that the crocodile seeks out and swallows, called gastroliths, bang into the food to break it up. Then, in the rear stomach chamber, powerful acid, the strongest known in any vertebrate, works on the bone, skin, and hair. Very little is wasted. On average, crocodiles probably eat about fifty times a year, or about once a week. One crocodile meal can be 20 percent of its body weight. (This is like a 150-pound person eating 120 quarter-pound hamburgers.) Such a feast may take a crocodile a week to digest—if the temperature is high enough. When crocodiles are cold, their digestive system slows down. So crocodiles usually only eat on days when the temperature is between 77–95 degrees F (25–35˚C).

Crocodiles do not use all the energy from their food right away. They are able to store more than half of it as fat in their tails, backs, and abdomens. There are three reasons why so much of their food can be stored away: First, crocodiles do not use a lot of energy to hunt. Second, being cold-blooded, they do not need to use food to heat up their bodies. And third, their digestive system can break down bone, hair, and even tough, scaly skin. Because they can store so much of their food, large crocodiles can go for about two years without a meal. Being able to live for long periods between meals has surely been an advantage to the crocodile, in its long struggle to survive.

4 Master Hunters

As the setting sun melts into the marsh, an American crocodile slides on her belly down a muddy bank. Leaving the chilled air, she slips under a warm, wet blanket. With only her eyes and nose poking out, the crocodile floats, stretching out her four webbed feet for balance. A white egret stares down from a nearby tree. Her nest of white tufted chicks sits in the crook of tall branches. Suddenly, a cry disturbs the dusk. Flapping and squawking, a fluffy chick falls onto a shaky limb. The crocodile submerges. She holds her legs tightly against her body, but her tail weaves through the water like a strong snake. The crocodile stops at the base of the tree. With a swift twist of her tail, her massive body surges into the air. Seconds later, the marsh is still, except for one thin limb that is left empty and shuddering.

Across the world, in Tanzania, a Nile crocodile enjoys a snack of catfish. As he swallows his meal, a light dust begins to drift toward the pool. A faint rustling noise follows. The old crocodile knows this sound. He hears it once each year. The rustle swells into a thunderous, earthshaking crescendo. Thousands

A PUNY PREDATOR. THIS YOUNG NILE CROCODILE SILENTLY STALKS A HOVERING DRAGONFLY.

of bellowing wildebeest swarm toward the water on their annual migration. The thirsty wildebeest study the muddy shore. Then they begin, a few at a time, to take their first cautious sips. Occasionally they jerk up their heads and nervously back away from the bank. Drinking is always a dangerous time. Many land predators such as lions and hyenas hunt at these waterways.

After a while the wildebeest settle down and crowd the pool. Some animals are squeezed into deeper water. The old

LARGE NILE CROCODILES CAN HOLD THREE HUNDRED POUNDS OF STRUGGLING WILDEBEEST IN THEIR IRON GRIP.

crocodile, always watching, glides toward them. Peering above the water through two yellow eyes, he chooses his victim. Slipping beneath the surface he slithers through the muddy stream. When he is nose to nose with the wildebeest, the crocodile erupts from the water. In one graceful movement, he clamps his jaws around the wildebeest's neck, turns, and slides away from shore. The other wildebeest rear up and scatter, but soon they are back sipping at the waterhole. They do not stampede away, as they would from a known predator such as a leopard.

As the old crocodile latches onto his victim, the dead wildebeest's tail waves above the water like a flag. Two hooves appear; the horns bob up and float gently for an instant before sinking. Other crocodiles scramble down the banks and surge into the stream. The water boils with whirling crocodile bodies. Gripping the wildebeest, the crocodiles spin around, ripping into its flesh. The old crocodile surfaces with the wildebeest's neck and head in his mouth. Too big to swallow, he thrashes it against the water, breaking off a suitable-sized chunk. Then he tips his head and gulps it down. For now, the crocodiles will leave the wildebeest alone. They are too full to bring down more prey.

Fluid Movement

Crocodiles are still around after 200 million years, partly because they have mastered so many different ways of moving. This seems strange because crocodiles are famous for their lounging lifestyle. They do spend much of their time lying on land or floating in the water. But like all animals, crocodiles must move from place to place to stay alive. They must control their temperature, mate, build nests, escape danger, and hunt for food. The way they move depends upon their needs.

WITH A SUDDEN THRUST OF ITS POWERFUL TAIL, A CROCODILE CAN BLAST THROUGH THE WATER TO THREATEN OR SEIZE OTHER ANIMALS.

When crocodiles need to attack prey, they can blast into action. With just a quick twist of its tail, this reptile can rocket into the air. It doesn't even need a "running" start. From a floating position, the crocodile sweeps its tail in an s-shaped motion. This powerful push launches the reptile from the water in less than a second. Aiming perfectly, it engulfs birds and small mammals in its jaws. Hatchling crocodiles also capture prey this way, snapping up dragonflies and other insects from low-hanging branches. In fact, young crocodiles and small species use this technique more frequently than large animals. The heavier a crocodile, the harder it is to heave itself out of the water.

To swim, a crocodile uses the same s-shaped tail motion as it uses to leap from the water. Tucking its legs against its sleak body, the streamlined crocodile streaks through the water. To steer, the crocodile simply points its head in the right direction. The power of a crocodile's tail is important in propelling it, but its shape is crucial, too. A crocodile's tail is built like a paddle—long with wide, flat sides. With a swish of this strong, broad extension, a crocodile can leap into the air or race through a river.

In the water, a crocodile also relies on its legs and feet. When floating, it spreads all four legs to keep its balance. To steer and swim at slow speeds, it paddles with its front and rear feet. Crocodiles can also use their hind legs to launch surprise attacks. Hidden in shallow water, they swing their powerful tails and push with their hind legs, springing toward the bank to snatch unsuspecting animals from the shore.

Aquatic Adaptations

This stealthy leap is a crocodile's main method of catching land animals. Crocodiles are experts at sneaking up on their prey

THE MANY BITES ON THIS FISH ARE FROM THE CAIMAN JUGGLING THE FISH IN ITS MOUTH. CROCODILIANS MUST POSITION A FISH HEADFIRST, TO AVOID BEING INJURED BY ITS SHARP SPINES.

LOOKING NO MORE ALIVE THAN A FLOATING LOG, A SUBMERGED CROCODILE RELIES ON SURPRISE TO SNAG ITS PREY.

because their eyes, ears, and nose are located at the top of their heads. Like a submarine with only its periscope above the surface, they can survey without being seen. Crocodiles also rely on an excellent sense of smell. They have been known to locate an animal carcass that is a mile or two away from the water. When hunting in water, a crocodile's nostrils are usually the only part of the snout that is visible. They are perched on a small, round mound that pokes above the water like an island. When this "island" sinks, the nostrils automatically close to seal out the water.

A crocodile cannot seal its mouth the way it can seal its ears and nose. It has no lips, so water easily leaks in. When a crocodile is partly submerged to stalk prey, or is wrestling with an animal underwater, its mouth becomes flooded. Why doesn't it drown? Crocodiles have a "flood control" gate at the back of their mouths called the palatal valve. When this flap of skin closes, the mouth is sealed, thus preventing water from flowing into the throat and lungs. A crocodile's nostrils are connected to a long airway, which opens into the throat behind the palatal valve. So even with a mouthful of water, the crocodile can breathe if its nostrils are above the surface.

When a crocodile eats, muscles pull down the palatal valve, opening the throat. This means that crocodiles must enjoy their meals above the surface or water will enter their breathing passages. Sometimes crocodiles carry their prey onto land. At other times they simply raise their heads above water. Before eating, they toss the meat around in their mouth until it is positioned correctly. Then they flip their head back and count on gravity to swallow their prey. They do not have throat muscles to push the meal down.

WITHOUT MUSCLES FOR SWALLOWING, THIS CROCODILE WILL HAVE TO TOSS BACK ITS HEAD AND LET THE CHICKEN SLIDE DOWN ITS THROAT. FEATHERS, BONES, AND SCALY FEET WILL ALL BE DIGESTED IN THE CROCODILE'S ACIDIC STOMACH.

A Clever Predator

Crocodiles use another part of their body to catch and kill prey: their brain. Many crocodile behaviors connected with hunting and feeding show that these reptiles are intelligent and able to learn. Crocodiles are known to stalk their prey. They wait in water near popular animal trails, river crossings, or watering spots. They may also wait for days beneath the nests of waterbirds. If a chick falls from the nest or wanders onto low-hanging branches, the crocodiles are ready. In Australia, crocodiles station themselves below colonies of flying foxes. They wait until the foxes come down from the branches to drink, and then snap them up.

If a crocodile is not feeling patient, it may hunt more actively. The African slender-snouted crocodile uses its tail as a net to catch fish. It swims along the shore with its tail curved toward the bank. When enough fish have been gathered, the crocodile twists its head and scoops them up. Weaverbirds nest in reeds. Nile crocodiles sometimes catch a snack by bending the reeds back with their tails, flipping them forward and tossing hatchlings into the water.

Crocodiles will often cooperate with one another in their pursuit of food. In some parts of Africa, groups of crocodiles blockade the passage of migrating fish. They form a line or semicircle and snap at fish as they approach. The crocodiles don't fight over the fish; they stay in position, leaving no gaps in the lineup. Crocodiles also work together to handle larger prey too big to swallow. To get a bite-sized chunk of a big carcass, spinning in the water works well. But smaller animals rotate with the crocodile instead of staying put. To solve this problem, one crocodile holds the carcass in its jaws, while the other rolls around. Sometimes the two crocodiles spin on opposite sides of the carcass.

Tackling very large prey such as elephants and hippos also

LARGE GROUPS OF CROCODILES OFTEN GATHER WHERE FOOD IS ABUNDANT. THESE NILE CROCODILES ARE FEASTING ON A WILDEBEEST.

takes a group effort. In Zambia, 120 crocodiles were sighted converging on a dead hippopotamus. There was not enough room for all the crocodiles to feast at the same time, so they took turns. Forming a circle around the carcass, each crocodile moved in to twist off a piece. Then it swam to the edge of the circle to eat its share. Even with the great number of crocodiles and all the movement back and forth, no fighting broke out.

5 The Cycle of Life

A magnificent roar rumbles along the riverbank—the call of a kingly Nile crocodile. He has ruled this section of river for ten breeding seasons by defeating all who have dared to rival him. Daily he patrols his territory, permitting females to enter, but guarding against the intrusion of competing males. Paddling slowly through the water, he notices a younger crocodile—a male—slipping into the pool. The old crocodile raises his body above the water. His thick neck swells as he opens his strong jaws. Then he lifts off with his tail and streaks toward the invader, stirring up a storm of waves. The young male scrambles out of the pool, but not soon enough. As he retreats, he receives a sharp bite on the tip of his tail. The old crocodile, satisfied, backs up into his pool. He holds his head high above the water, watching his fleeing rival. Then the victorious old croc snaps his great jaws, smacking them hard against the water's surface. A blast of sound and spray explodes into the air.

THIS SQUEAKING 10-INCH (25-CM) NILE HATCHLING MAY GROW TO BE A ROARING REPTILE TWENTY TIMES ITS PRESENT LENGTH.

The sound seems to echo along the riverbank, as his signal is picked up and repeated by other crocodiles. One crocodile who hears is a female. She approaches the large male, exposing the underside of her throat. The old crocodile understands this silent language. He submerges and begins blowing a foamy film of bubbles in the water. Next he swims around her, circling several times. Coming in closer, he rubs his snout against hers. The young female nuzzles in return. Then the big crocodile sinks below the female and lifts her partly out of the water.

When the male surfaces, he continues to court the female by stroking his jaws and throat against her head and back. Scent glands on the underside of the male's jaws release an oily musk, which perfumes the air and water. The female raises her head above the water to show her acceptance of the courting male. Slightly opening her jaws, she makes a soft, purring growl. This is the first time this female has accepted the old crocodile as a mate. For days he has tried unsuccessfully to woo her. Meanwhile, he has courted and mated with five other females in his territory. For the remainder of the breeding season, he will continue to mate with other females.

The Nesting Site

After mating, the young female searches for a suitable spot to lay her eggs. Searching along the shore, she comes to a sandy site bathed in warm sunlight. Located far from the high water mark, it appears to be safe from flooding. It is also near a hippopotamus trail. This path will make getting down to the water easier when the hatchlings are born. Suddenly there is the sound of twigs snapping and the rustling of leaves. A large female crocodile crawls into the clearing.

The younger female stands firmly in the sand and growls a

greeting. A spirited roar is the older crocodile's answer. The battle begins. Raising up on their front legs, the two females meet, shoulder to shoulder. Pushing against each other, they wrestle in the sand. The young female snaps at the older one, trying to nip the back of her neck. The older crocodile is larger and heavier than the young female. With a quick flip, she overpowers her smaller rival. Defeated, the young crocodile crawls away. Although Nile crocodiles may nest communally in crowded areas, this young female must search for another nesting place. The following day, she decides upon a site that is open and sunny. It is closer to the water than the other area, but it is more elevated, which should protect it from high water.

One warm night, a few weeks after mating, the young crocodile is ready to begin digging out her nest. Sand flies as she shovels out the dirt with her claws and the wide webbing on her strong back feet. Finally, when her hind legs fit all the way into the hole, she stops. Crawling forward over the hollow, she begins to lay her eggs. As each egg drops into the pit, she cradles it with her hind feet. During the next hour, she will lay forty white-shelled eggs. Years from now, when she is older and larger, she will lay twice as many. (Some small species, such as the dwarf crocodile, may lay fewer than twenty.) When her eggs are deposited, the young crocodile covers them with sand, leaving no trace of the huge hole. As a finishing touch, the crocodile rubs her lower jaw back and forth over the sand. This marks the site with oil from her scent glands.

The Extraordinary Egg

Forty eggs now lie safely beneath the soil. They are slightly bigger than chicken eggs, but not as brittle. There is a leathery lining under the white, chalky shell. Tucked inside each egg is a growing

For three months a mother Nile crocodile guards her buried eggs, barely eating and leaving only to drink. The yelps of her hatchlings tell her it is time to dig them out.

crocodile embryo. These embryos are not yet male or female. Their gender will be determined by the temperature inside the nest. Under very warm or cool conditions, the embryos will become female. Temperatures in between produce mostly males. Sometimes different layers within a nest are not the same temperature, and both males and females will hatch.

Until they hatch, the embryos have everything they need inside their egg. They can breathe because small openings in the shell allow oxygen to seep in. When the embryo breathes out, carbon dioxide leaves the egg and enters the nest chamber. There it reacts with moisture in the air to form a weak acid. This acid coats the egg and may thin out the shell, making it easier for the baby to hatch. The acid may also increase the size of the pores in the shell. So as the embryo grows, it can receive more oxygen.

In order to grow, the embryo needs food. Each egg is provided with a packet of food called the yolk sac. Waste from the food that is digested is stored in another sac, called the allantois. Each embryo also has a little water bed—a fluid-filled sac that surrounds the growing crocodile. This watery cushion protects the embryo from jostling and helps to keep it from drying out. Moisture, though, rather than dryness, is more often the enemy. Under

WHENEVER A NILE CROCODILE LEAVES HER NEST FOR A DRINK, SHE RUNS THE RISK OF A PREDATOR RAIDING HER NEST. IN MOST SEASONS ABOUT HALF HER EGGS WILL BE EATEN.

damp conditions, eggs may become infected with fungus. Gases from the rotting eggs will poison the healthy ones. And always there is the danger of drowning from flooding and heavy rains.

Nest Defense

After padding down the soil, the mother crocodile lies over her nest. Although she cannot save her eggs from flood or drought, there are many ways she can protect them. For three full months she remains near her nest, barely eating. One hot afternoon, she lumbers from her nest to rest in the shade. A tall marabou stork wanders up the beach. As it strolls, it pokes its bill into the sand, searching for eggs. When it approaches the crocodile's nest, the young mother rushes toward him, sending the startled stork flapping away.

The heat of the day has made the crocodile thirsty, so she crawls over the sand for a gulp of water. A monitor lizard, hidden in the bushes, scurries toward the nest. Her long, forked tongue flickers in and out as she digs furiously at the dirt. The drinking crocodile does not see the lizard. But as soon as the mother heads for her nest, the lizard dashes away—with an egg in her mouth.

The next day is warm again, but wet. The rain pelts down on the crocodile, who faithfully shields her eggs. She lies over them like a scaly umbrella. When the rain ends, a soft-shelled turtle paddles through the sand. The crocodile tries to grab her, but she escapes into the water. The turtle will return another day to dig her nest on this shore. The eggs that she lays and leaves will be protected by the mother crocodile, who keeps away egg-eaters. Weaverbirds that nest near crocodiles also receive protection. A colony of black and yellow weavers have built their basket-like nests in a tree by the shore. The crocodile stands guard nearby.

During the morning she chases away a monitor lizard and scares off a snake—two animals that prey on weaver nests.

Soon the weavers' eggs begin to hatch, and the nests are noisy with baby chicks. The parents squeeze through the narrow holes in the bottom of the nest, delivering food. One young chick, exploring outside the nest, totters on a limb and falls into the water. Flapping its small wings, it scoots through the pool. The mother crocodile plunges in and catches the chick in her jaws. This has been her first food in weeks. Although this chick has died, the rest of the colony has been kept safe.

Many soft-shelled turtle eggs that were laid nearby are also hatching. Batches of baby turtles scramble toward the water. One baby pauses near the snout of the mother crocodile. The mother picks it up with her teeth, flips it into her mouth, and heads for the water. Swimming into the pool, she opens her jaws, and the tiny turtle swims away.

Helping the Hatchlings

About three months after laying her eggs, the female crocodile is greeted by squeaking sounds coming from her nest. Hurrying across the sand, she begins to dig. She uses her front feet, and sometimes her teeth, to snip at roots that have grown between the eggs. She does not dig as skillfully as the monitor lizard, and must pause often to rest. As she works, the squeaking grows louder.

When the first eggs are uncovered, some babies have already broken free. They were able to split open their shells using a piece of spiky skin at the top of their snouts. This temporary tool is called an "egg tooth", or caruncle. The mother crocodile lowers her head into the nest and picks up a wriggling hatchling with her teeth. Sensors at the base of each tooth allow her to feel the baby so she will not press too hard and hurt the hatchling. With

LEFT: BREAKING OUT OF ITS EGG IS AN ARDUOUS TASK FOR A HATCHLING. A SHARP SPIKE OF SKIN AT THE TIP OF ITS SNOUT HELPS IT CUT THROUGH THE SHELL.

RIGHT: THIS CURLED-UP HATCHLING WILL SOON BE FREE OF ITS CRAMPED QUARTERS.

the little baby dangling from her teeth, she tosses her mouth, flipping the hatchling into her mouth.

Other babies are still struggling and squeaking inside their eggs. The mother picks them up, too. Gently, she squeezes each unhatched egg in her mouth. After several minutes, the baby slithers free. With tiny heads and tails poking out between her teeth, the crocodile walks toward the water. About a dozen hatchlings squirm inside the pouch at the bottom of her mouth. In the pool, the mother searches for a shallow section filled with weeds. Then she opens her mouth and slowly shakes her head. Egg shells and hatchlings float out into the water.

Back at the nest, a banquet has begun. The squeaking babies have alerted others besides the mother. A big baboon has grabbed an egg and is sitting atop a tree, fussily brushing off the sand. When the egg is clean enough, the baboon begins gnawing at it with its front teeth. A furry black marsh mongoose stands by the nest on its hind legs. Repeatedly, it drops an egg on the ground, trying to break it. Finally the egg cracks, and the mongoose bites the shell with its small, sharp teeth. When the mother crocodile returns, she finds a monitor lizard making off with a baby in its mouth. Hurrying to escape, the lizard drops the baby. Seconds later, a fish eagle swoops down and soars away with the hatchling clutched in its talons.

The mother crocodile makes two more trips to the water

PEOPLE USED TO THINK THAT CROCODILE MOTHERS ATE THEIR EGGS. BUT BY ROLLING THEM GENTLY IN HER MOUTH, THIS FEMALE IS ACTUALLY CRACKING THE SHELLS.

THE CROCODILE MOTHER IN BACK IS FLIPPING HER HATCHLING INTO HER MOUTH SO
SHE CAN CARRY IT DOWN TO THE WATER.

before her nest is empty. Although the nest is no longer filled
with crocodile eggs, it will soon contain eggs of another kind.
Kingfishers dive at the inside wall of the nest, dashing into it with
their pointy orange bills. When the hole is big enough, the birds
squirm in and scratch out more sand with their feet. Soon baby
kingfishers will be hatching here. The crocodile egg shells,
strewn around on the sand, will become the egg shells of various birds. Swallows and starlings eat the crumpled shells, which
give them the needed calcium to make their own eggs. In the
water, the scent of the discarded shells has attracted fish. They
nip and nibble at the membranes still attached to the shell.

Hidden in the weeds in the shallow water, the hatchlings are now safer than on the sand. But there are many predators here, too, so the babies stick close to their mother. When she surfaces, they climb onto her head to bask. She looks like she is wearing a strange hat. The little hatchlings still squeak a lot. Hearing each other's calls helps them stay together. It also makes it easier for their mother to keep track of them. One hatchling wanders into deeper water where there are no weeds to conceal it. Catfish and huge Nile perch, weighing 100 pounds (45 kg), cruise these waters. The innocent hatchling, swimming slowly along, heads straight into the cavelike mouth of a giant perch.

Another baby, who strays from the nursery, is luckier. The father crocodile, who remains in the area, hears the squeaking hatchling and carries it to the mother in his jaws. As he releases

THIS HATCHLING HAS FOUND THE SAFEST BASKING SITE AROUND.

the baby, he notices a fish eagle circling over the water. The mother crocodile also notices. She quickly vibrates the muscles of her upper body, making waves that send the hatchlings diving for cover. When the fish eagle flies lower, the father leaps up, snapping his jaws. The eagle glides away, and the mother submerges with her hatchlings. Then they all pop up, and the babies scramble for a spot on top of their mother.

Even with their parents' protection, only eight hatchlings are still alive after a few weeks. Many predators hunt these babies, but now the babies must learn to be hunters, too. One hatchling sinks low in the water, stalking a dragonfly on a twig. Floating in quietly, the hatchling springs up and snatches the insect in her small jaws. As a 10-inch (25-cm) hatchling, insects,

SOME WILDLIFE MANAGEMENT SPECIALISTS ESTIMATE THAT 90 PERCENT OF HATCHLING CROCODILES DO NOT SURVIVE THEIR FIRST YEAR.

tadpoles, small frogs, and fish are about all she can manage. But all the while she is honing her hunting skills—diving, leaping, and of course, being stealthy.

Crocodile Communication

A male crocodile is defending his territory, a female is ready to mate, and a baby is struggling to hatch. What do all these crocodiles have in common? They all need to communicate. Throughout the days, crocodiles must communicate with each other to survive. Like people, they use body language, sounds, touch, and odor. Also like people, some of their signals may have more than one meaning. For instance if someone slaps you on the back, that person could be congratulating you or starting a fight. Although the action is the same, you have no difficulty knowing what the person means. Crocodiles are also skillful at decoding each other's signs. Below is a list of some of the signals that crocodiles regularly use.

Vocalizations. Crocodile vocalizations include the squeaks of hatchlings and the roars, bellows, and growls of grown-ups. A baby squeaking inside its egg is telling its mother, "I'm ready to hatch!" The mother responds to its call by digging up the nest. When a hatchling wanders away from the nursery, its squeaky call may be saying, "Where is everybody?" Other crocodiles, even those which are not parents, will respond by returning the hatchling. A bellowing adult crocodile may want to announce, "This is my territory!" Or it may be saying, "I'm over here. Is anyone else around?" Other crocodiles will usually bellow an answer in return. Researchers have found that crocodile species living in swampy or marshy areas vocalize more often than those living in open areas. This is probably because they can't see each other, so they call to keep in touch.

A LOOK INSIDE THESE CROCODILES' THROATS SHOWS WHERE THE PALATAL VALVE MEETS THE BACK OF THE TONGUE. TO EAT, CROCODILES MUST OPEN THIS VALVE.

Headslapping and Exhalations. When the breeding season starts, adult crocodiles begin defending their territories, courting, and mating. Their impressive headslapping is most noticeable at these times. To headslap, a crocodile snaps its mouth shut, slapping its lower jaw against the water. The loud snapping and splashing sound that this makes reaches other crocodiles, who usually headslap back. Researchers can recognize individual crocodiles from the unique way each one headslaps. Other crocodiles can probably recognize one another, too. So headslapping may be a way for crocodiles to form a group and to keep it together.

After headslapping, crocodiles will often exhale air into the water from their throat and nostrils. In other words, they blow bubbles. They may blow a gentle stream of small bubbles or big exploding ones. Crocodiles also exhale air from their nostrils while on land to make a hissing sound.

Body Language. The dominant croc in an area lets everyone know how important he is by his body language. He swims at the water's surface showing off most of his large body. When other crocodiles swim by him, they keep only their heads above water. To avoid a fight, they must let him know that they realize he is superior. They do this by snout lifting—raising their snouts to him and exposing their unprotected throats. Tail thrashing is a sign that a crocodile may want to fight. Raising his tail above water, the crocodile whips it from side to side. He may also wag his tail on land as a sign of aggression.

Odor. Crocodiles also communicate with odor coded messages using their four scent glands. One pair of glands is located under the chin. The other pair is in the cloaca near the tail. These glands release a musky oil that even young crocodiles seem able to smell. Scientists are not sure how crocodiles communicate with this oil. But from their studies with other reptiles, researchers think crocodiles may use the musk for several purposes. Their scent may scare away predators, mark their territory, and help them find mates.

THE CROCODILE ON THE RIGHT MAY LOOK THREATENING, BUT IT IS PROBABLY JUST COOLING OFF BY LETTING MOISTURE EVAPORATE FROM ITS MOUTH.

6 Species Portraits

American Crocodile

Crocodylus acutus

Habitat: Fresh or partly salty (brackish) water near coastal areas
Distribution: Southern Florida, southern Mexico, Caribbean
    Islands, Central America, northern South America
Maximum size: 19.5 feet (6 m)

There are about five hundred American crocodiles living in Florida, but you probably won't ever see one. American crocodiles stay away from people and try to avoid being spotted. They usually succeed. Crocodiles can hear the vibrations of people walking, have good eyesight, and are experts in the art of camouflage. But when an 11-foot (3-m) crocodile lays forty-seven eggs in your garden, it's hard not to notice. Residents of a

AMERICAN CROCODILE. THIS CROCODILE IS TIMID AND RARELY SEEN BY PEOPLE. HOWEVER ITS NEIGHBOR, THE AMERICAN ALLIGATOR, OFTEN APPEARS IN BACKYARDS AND SWIMMING POOLS.

Florida neighborhood worked together to protect their nesting crocodile, whom they called Wilma. They left her alone and blocked off the street each night so she could cross safely. Local reporters also helped by keeping her nest a secret. To everyone's disappointment, Wilma's eggs never hatched. But people have piled sand in their yards in hopes that she will try again another year.

One area where American crocodiles have made many successful nests is near a nuclear power plant. When Florida Power and Light Company (FPL) built 168 miles (270 km) of cooling canals, the crocodiles came. Females found that the piles of peat left over from digging the canals made great nesting sites. Because no one is allowed into the nesting area without FPL's permission, the skittish mothers and their nests are not disturbed.

Crocodile mothers stay with their eggs, unlike turtles and other reptiles. At hatching time, when the mother hears squeaky calls, she digs up the earth and releases her noisy brood. Most of these little hatchlings will become meals for birds, raccoons, otters, crabs, and fish. But some young will survive and grow up to eat the creatures that snacked on their siblings.

Nile Crocodile

Crocodylus niloticus
Habitat: Freshwater rivers, lakes, marshes, and swamps, as well as brackish coastal areas
Distribution: South of the Sahara Desert in Africa and Madagascar
Maximum size: 19.5 feet (6 m)

The Nile crocodile could really be called the Nile-Ubangi-Zambezi crocodile because the Nile River is not its only home. Many wetland areas south of the Sahara Desert shelter this crocodile. Due to a change in climate toward drier conditions, its range is shrinking. However, dams that people have built in some areas have changed the water levels, helping the crocodile. In 1972, there were no Nile crocodiles in Egypt. But since the building of the Aswan Dam, crocodiles are returning.

The Nile crocodile is not like its American relatives which shy away from people. Of all the crocodiles, the Nile is one of the most aggressive. It needs a fierce personality to survive because its habitat is home to so many kinds of competitors. These range from sharks and other crocodile species to small mongooses who eat crocodile eggs. For thousands of years people have lived—and died—with the Nile crocodile. Even today, many people in Africa wade into rivers to fish, swim, and wash clothes. About three hundred of these people are killed each year by this predator. But encounters between crocodiles and humans are not always fatal. In Zimbabwe, a crocodile decided that it liked living in the water on the sixth hole of a golf course. This was fine with the golfers, as long as they didn't have to fetch their lost balls.

Although the Nile crocodile fearlessly pursues people, there are some animals from which it usually keeps a respectful distance. One such beast is the powerful hippopotamus. Crocodiles and hippos often share the same water holes. There is usually no trouble, unless a crocodile attempts to turn a baby hippo into a meal. Furious female hippos, protecting their young, have grabbed and crushed crocodiles in their gigantic jaws. Encounters with elephants can also be deadly for this reptile. About one hundred and fifty years ago, people witnessed a Nile crocodile latch onto the leg of an elephant. The elephant bolted out of the water, hauling the crocodile behind it. Another elephant came to the rescue by stomping on the crocodile.

Then the injured elephant grabbed the dead crocodile with its trunk, and flung it into a tree.

Other animals that appear to have no fear of the Nile crocodile are little birds such as the spur-winged plover, the thick-knee, and the ziczac. For over two thousand years, people have reported seeing these birds hopping around on the crocodile's back and even in its mouth. The birds are picking at parasites and nibbling on leftover food between the crocodile's teeth.

NILE CROCODILE. HATCHLINGS STAY IN QUIET WATERS WHERE THEY FEED ON INSECTS AND SMALL FROGS. THEIR PARENTS PROTECT THEM FOR UP TO TWO MONTHS.

They also eat leeches, which attach to the soft skin inside the crocodile's mouth. This cleaning job keeps the crocodiles happy and also feeds the birds.

Indo-Pacific Crocodile

Crocodylus porosus
Habitat: Freshwater rivers, lakes, marshes, and swamps, brackish
    coastal areas, and marine habitats
Distribution: Tropical areas of Asia and the Pacific Ocean
Maximum size: 23 feet (7 m)

The Indo-Pacific crocodile is often called "salty" or "saltwater crocodile" because it sometimes drifts in the ocean to islands that are more than 800 miles (1,280 km) from the mainland. How does the Indo-Pacific crocodile survive without fresh water? Like all crocodiles, it has special salt glands on its tongue. When its body fluids become overloaded with salt, these glands secrete droplets of salty liquid.

Besides being famous for these ocean voyages, the Indo-Pacific crocodile is known as the biggest and fiercest crocodile in the world. Individuals have grown to be more than 23 feet (7 m) long. Balanced on their tails, the tips of their snouts would reach a second story window. These large crocs often weigh over 2,000 pounds (900 kg). Hatchlings, however, weigh much less than human babies. Each hatchling weighs only about 2 ounces (57 g). But when it grows up, it will be the biggest reptile on Earth.

Many places in the world are home to this crocodile. In fact, it is the most widely ranging of all the species. Its broad distribution, combined with its aggressive nature, leads to the death of about 1,000 people each year. Nevertheless, tourists are attracted

INDO-PACIFIC CROCODILE. THIS CROCODILE IS COMMONLY CALLED AN ESTUARINE, OR SALTWATER, CROCODILE. BUT SINCE IT IS OFTEN FOUND IN FRESHWATER LAKES AND RIVERS, ITS NAME IS MISLEADING.

to places such as northern Australia, where over 60,000 of these reptiles reside.

Since northern Australia's temperature is often in the nineties, people are out swimming, fishing, and boating despite the crocodiles. A fisherman cleaning his fish in a creek reported that a 10-foot (3-m) crocodile snatched his catch. Elsewhere, a large male crocodile, named "Sweetheart," regularly attacked motorboats entering his territory. He always ignored the people jumping overboard, but continued to bump the boat. Scientists have begun experimenting with relocating crocodiles to less populated areas, but the crocodiles do not always cooperate. One journeyed 19 miles (30 km) over land and water to return home.

American Alligator

Alligator mississippiansis
Habitat: Mostly swamps and marshes
Distribution: Southeastern United States
Maximum size: 14.5 feet (4 m)

When Spanish explorers came to North America, they had never seen an alligator. They named the creature *el lagarto* (Spanish for lizard) after the little reptiles they had seen in Europe. Like crocodiles, alligators cannot live in the cold European climate, but they can live in colder places than crocodiles. Both species of alligator live in areas where the winter temperature may drop below freezing for short periods of time. How do they survive?

Although crocodiles slow down their body systems when they are cold, they are not true hibernators like snakes and frogs. Scientists have discovered that when the temperature drops below freezing, alligators head for shallow waters. There they lie with just the tip of their nose sticking out of the water. The rest of their long body lies in warmer, deeper water. Even if the water freezes around them, they can stay alive with their nose poking out of the ice. Alligators have been able to survive cold spells where their body temperature has dropped to as low as 41 degrees F (5° C). But if a warm winter day comes along, they perk right up.

Besides surviving the cold, alligators also have to make it through the dry season each year. They do so by digging deep holes that remain filled with water until the rains return. Animals

AMERICAN ALLIGATOR. UNLIKE CROCODILES, ALLIGATORS DO NOT HAVE SALT GLANDS, SO THEY ARE DRAWN TO FRESHWATER HABITATS.

such as fish and birds take refuge in these gator holes. Some of them are eaten by the alligator, but others can thank the gator for their survival.

Cuvier's Dwarf Caiman

Paleosuchus palpebrosus
Habitat: Flooded forests near large lakes and rivers, and fast-flowing waterways
Distribution: Northern South America, from the Orinco and Amazon river basins into the Paraguay river system
Maximum size: 5 feet (1.5 m)

Cuvier's dwarf caiman is the smallest of all the crocodilians. But what this caiman lacks in size, it makes up for in armor. Both its back and belly skin are heavily fortified with osteoderms. No other crocodilian has as much bony protection. Because of their small size, these caimans may need a tough hide to deter would-be predators. Layers of osteoderms also shield them from rocks and sharp branches in the rushing waters that they frequent.

CUVIER'S DWARF CAIMAN. WITH ITS DOGLIKE SKULL, THIS CROCODILIAN IS NOTICEABLY DIFFERENT FROM THE OTHERS.

When they wander from the water, this bony casing offers protection against both land predators and obstacles.

Cuvier's dwarf caimans venture onto land quite often. During the day they rest in burrows. At night, adults commonly roam large distances from the water. The fact that they are not as aquatic as most crocodilians may be the reason for their unique shaped skull. Other crocodilians have a long, flat, streamlined head. This shape offers little resistance when slicing through water. Cuvier's dwarf caiman, however, has a short, upturned snout and a high forehead.

Gharials

Gavialis gangeticus
Habitat: Deep, fast-flowing rivers
Distribution: Northern part of Indian subcontinent
Maximum size: 19.5–2.5 feet (6–7 m)

Gharials are the "Pinocchios" of the crocodilians, with their long, skinny snouts. Because of their narrow jaws they cannot crush turtle shells as do the broad-snouted alligators. Nor do they wrestle with the large mammals that similar-sized crocodilians eat. Gharials mostly hunt for fish by swinging their slender snouts sideways through the water. They grip the fish with needle-sharp teeth, so that their prey doesn't slip away.

Gharials were once believed to eat people because rings and bracelets were discovered in their stomachs. This is probably because people in the region have the religious custom of floating bodies down the river. Gharials may snap up the jewelry from the water, just as they swallow other hard objects such as stones. These gastroliths remain in the stomach, where they help grind the gharials' food.

The gharial got its name from the fancy snout found only on the male. At the tip of the adult male's nose is a round, fleshy bulb. This bump reminded people of an Indian pot called a ghara. During mating season, males make a buzzing noise with this bulb. The sound may be used to scare other males away and to attract females.

GHARIALS ARE DESIGNED FOR LIFE IN THE WATER. THEIR FEET ARE WEBBED, AND THEIR LEG MUSCLES ARE TOO WEAK TO CARRY THEM VERY FAR ON LAND.

7 Conservation

As a glowing sun sets on the Everglades, two researchers head out in their motorboat. In the bay, peach-colored waters swirl around them—as do whirring mosquitoes. Soon, the man and woman leave the open waters and enter a creek choked with mangrove trees. Tangled roots block the boat's passage, and the scientists must cut their way through the maze.

Inching forward, they search the branches and roots with flashlights. There! Reflected in the beams are dozens of sparkling eyes sprinkled across the water. These are the eyes of American crocodile hatchlings. Wading into the water, the researchers pick up handfuls of the 10-inch (25-cm) hatchlings, fifteen in all. Back at their camp, the scientists record the babies' weights and lengths. Then they clip a number of the raised scales on each crocodile's tail. These clippings allow them to identify each crocodile the next time they find it.

From their research, these scientists have learned much

IN THE 1960S, CROCODILE FARMS WERE SET UP IN CUBA TO CONSERVE THE CUBAN CROCODILE. THIS SPECIES IS HIGHLY ENDANGERED; IT HAS THE SMALLEST WILD POPULATION OF ANY CROCODILIAN.

RADIO COLLARS ON THESE TINY AMERICAN CROCODILES WILL HELP SCIENTISTS IN THE EVERGLADES LEARN MORE ABOUT THEIR HABITS AND MOVEMENTS.

about crocodiles. They know that the American crocodile is fast growing, and may double its length in the first year. They have also discovered that the female often returns to the same nesting spot each breeding season. Learning as much as they can about crocodiles is necessary for scientists to be able to protect them. But not everyone who searches for crocodiles is trying to save them. Poachers still hunt many endangered species.

On a river in India, a white moon glitters like a spotlight on the black water. Floating on the surface is a small wooden boat. Quietly it glides to the sound of splashing paddles. At the front of the boat sits a hunter with a harpoon. Another man, in back, has a flashlight, a knife, and an axe. Letting the boat slide to a stop, he aims his flashlight at the weeds. A big mugger crocodile hides in the tangled marsh, watching the boat. The other hunter cups his hands to his mouth. A shrill squeaking sound, like a frightened hatchling, rips through the marsh. The big crocodile raises his head. Then he snaps his jaws and slams them against the water. Fearlessly, he lunges toward the boat, but his fierce yellow eyes are caught by the light. Guided by these glowing disks, the hunter hurls his harpoon. It tears through the reeds and stops, buried inside its target.

Killing Crocodiles

Why do people hunt crocodiles? For thousands of years, people have eaten crocodile meat. Crocodiles have also been hunted for their body parts. In many cultures, their internal organs are prized as medicine. Today their bones and osteoderms are added to animal feed to improve its nutritional value. Even their musk and urine have been used to make perfume. People have also killed crocodiles out of fear, thinking that it was good to destroy such dangerous beasts. And like other large predators, crocodiles have been hunted for sport. Their decorated skulls were placed in homes as religious shrines, and ancient magicians added their teeth and claws to potions.

Today tourists buy crocodile teeth, claws, and hatchling skulls as souvenirs. Briefcases, shoes, and wallets made from crocodile hides sell for hundreds and thousands of dollars. These luxury items are the main reason people hunt crocodiles today. About $2 billion dollars worth of crocodile products are sold each year throughout the world.

Often, however, people kill crocodiles indirectly. As the human population grows, our need for food, housing, and materials increases. This leads to a decrease in the crocodile population.

For example, waste water from gold or copper mines is sometimes dumped into lakes and rivers where crocodiles live. This pollutes the wetland, causing crocodiles in that area to die. Problems for crocodiles also occur when people cut canals through waterways and build roads along rivers. These routes bring humans and crocodiles into closer contact, disturbing crocodiles and perhaps scaring them away from their nests. More access also makes for easier hunting.

Even though crocodiles do not live in the woods, our increasing need for trees cuts down on the number of crocodiles. Without trees to anchor the soil, silt is swept into streams. Clogged with silt, they cannot hold as much water for fish and other animals that crocodiles eat. This means fewer crocodiles. Besides holding down soil, forests also hold water. After it rains, water is stored in the roots, stems, and leaves of plants. Without the forest, this water rushes directly into rivers. This may cause flooding and destruction of nests.

Crocodiles also suffer when wetlands are drained and filled for housing and farmland. This destroys crocodile habitat. Unfortunately, habitat near these areas is affected as well because farms and cities take water from rivers. Less fresh water flows into wetlands, and the water that remains may become too salty.

Crocodile Connections

When crocodile numbers decline because of overhunting or lost habitat, the effects ripple out like waves from a tossed stone. Many creatures—including humans—are connected to crocodiles. Crocodile eggs provide food for various kinds of animals. These range from raccoons to coyotes, and from warthogs to hyenas. Other animals, such as ravens, leopards, and herons, eat the hatchlings. Many birds and fish find crocodile egg shells appetizing. When crocodiles disappear, there is less food for all these creatures. Other animals that benefit from the presence of crocodiles are soft-shelled turtles and weaverbirds. By laying their eggs near these guardians of the beach, their nests are better protected and more successful.

When crocodile populations began to disappear, people were surprised at the results. Fishers, who figured they'd be better off without these fish-eating competitors, were disappointed. Their catches actually declined. One reason for this may be that large predators such as crocodiles feed and then excrete waste into the water. This recycles the nutrients for smaller animals such as fish. More nutrients increases the fish population. Another reason fishers experienced a loss may be that crocodiles hunt fish that prey on the kind people catch. With crocodiles around, there are fewer predators eating the fish people want. Crocodiles are beneficial to fish because they open up paths in marshy waterways, and they deepen pools, which helps keep water available during the dry season. No wonder many fishers prefer to fish with the crocodile.

Conserving the Crocodile

In the late 1960's, people became alarmed; many species of crocodile were becoming extinct. Nations passed laws to protect the crocodiles in their countries, but hunters still killed crocodiles illegally. These skins were then sold to smugglers, who would sneak them out of the country. As long as people in other countries continued to buy these hides, the poaching continued.

Real progress in conserving crocodiles did not begin until 1973. That year, representatives met at an international conference in Washington, D.C. where they drafted the Convention on International Trade on Endangered Species (CITES). The convention requires that participating nations prohibit the trade of endangered species. Representatives created two lists: the first with the names of endangered species and the second with those species that are not yet endangered but likely to become so if trade is not carefully monitored.

How do CITES nations know which crocodile species are endangered? How do they find out when a species is doing better and can be taken off the endangered list? CITES nations rely on organizations such as the Crocodile Specialist Group (CSG) to give them advice. The CSG is part of the International Union

THESE THREE-YEAR-OLD CROCODILES ARE BEING REARED ON A FARM IN THAILAND, WHERE TIN-MINING OPERATIONS HAVE DESTROYED CROCODILE HABITAT.

for the Conservation of Nature (IUCN). This organization has members around the world who work in many ways to prevent crocodilian extinction. They encourage countries to manage and conserve crocodilians and their habitats. They also work directly with crocodiles by conducting surveys of wild populations and doing research on their behavior and ecology. Keeping an eye on trade is another job of the CSG. Since their experts know the differences among species, they can identify legal and illegal skins and products.

With the CSG and CITES working together, poaching and smuggling have begun to decline. Countries who export crocodile products, and countries who receive them, must now keep records. This way officials can detect illegal trade when the number of crocodile products going out does not match the number coming in. Illegal trade has also been slowed by printing export permits on security paper. This paper has a complicated background pattern that is difficult to counterfeit and will smear easily if changes are made. Non-removable plastic tags have also thwarted poachers and smugglers. These are placed on legal hides, with information about the species and country of origin.

Besides monitoring trade, people have begun protecting crocodiles by preserving and restoring their habitat. Habitat is preserved when parks and wildlife refuges are set aside. Habitat is restored by replanting wetlands. Crocodiles can be brought into these restored areas from conservation and educational farms. On these farms, endangered crocodile species are bred with the intention of releasing them into protected wild areas.

Other types of farms breed crocodiles for the purpose of selling their skins. Ranches also raise crocodiles for this reason. Ranches are different from farms in that the crocodiles they raise were not born there. They were taken as eggs or juveniles from the wild.

WHEN THIS "LOG" DECIDES TO DIVE, THE BASKING TURTLE WILL BE IN FOR A SURPRISE.

Though farms and ranches have increased the number of some species of endangered crocodiles, captive breeding cannot replace wild populations. Large natural populations have a greater variety of genes than small captive ones. This diversity makes the species more adaptable. Also, captive crocodiles do not play the same ecological role as their free-roaming relatives. Crocodiles on farms and ranches do not help starlings or coyotes, fish eagles or fishers. We are just now uncovering all the crocodile connections. Ancient Egyptians, who lived closely with crocodiles, honored this reptile. They connected the crocodile with well-being. Today, thousands of years later, we are finding out how right they were.

Glossary

amphibious—capable of living both on land and in water

aquatic—living or growing in water

archosaurs—the "ruling reptiles" that lived during the Mesozoic era (245–65 million years ago), including the crocodilians, the dinosaurs, the pterosaurs, and the thecodontians

atrium (plural atria)—one of the upper chambers of the heart

calcium—an element found in teeth, bones, shells, and limestone

camouflage—to conceal oneself by blending into the background through the use of color, shape, or pattern

carnivore—a meat-eating organism

caruncle—a temporary sharp spike of skin on a hatchling crocodile's snout, used for breaking out of the egg

classification—a system for living organisms includes seven levels: kingdom, phylum, class, order, family, genus, and species

cloaca—the cavity into which the intestinal, genital, and urinary tracts open in crocodilians

ecology—the branch of biology concerned with the relationship between an organism and its environment

ectothermic—an animal that cannot produce its own body heat and must rely on external sources

embryo—an organism in the early stages of development

endangered—threatened with extinction

estuary—area where a freshwater river meets the ocean tides

eusuchian—the group of crocodilians that first appeared about 80 million years ago, to which modern crocodilians belong

evolve—to change over time

extinct—no longer existing

fossil—the remains or traces of an organism

gastroliths—stones swallowed by crocodilians that help break up the food in the stomach

genes—molecules that encode for the structure and functioning of an organism, and are passed from parent to offspring

habitat—the place where an organism lives, including the nonliving environment and the other organisms that live in the environment

herbivore—a plant-eating animal

keratin—the tough protein that forms the outer layer of a crocodilian's scales

mammal—a class of warm-blooded vertebrates that have fur or hair and feed their babies milk

mesosuchians—the group of crocodilians that first appeared about 190 million years ago; they represent the middle stage of crocodilian evolution

nictitating membrane—a transparent third eyelid that covers the eye when a crocodilian submerges

osteoderms—bony plates embedded in crocodilian skin

palatal valve—a flap of skin at the back of a crocodilian's mouth that can close to separate the mouth from the throat

parasite—an organism that lives on or in another organism, but does nothing to contribute to the survival of its host

plankton—microscopic plants and animals that drift in fresh or saltwater

poikilothermic—animals whose body temperature varies with the environment

predator—an animal that hunts and eats other animals

protosuchians—the group of crocodilians that first appeared about 215 million years ago; they represent the earliest stage of crocodilian evolution

reptile—a class of cold-blooded vertebrates with lungs and scales

scavenger—an animal that feeds on dead or decaying matter

species—the basic category of biological classification, designating a single kind of organism

tapetum— a light reflecting layer at the back of the crocodilian eye

taxonomist—a scientist who deals with classification

terrestrial—living on land

thecodontian—socket-toothed reptiles from which the archosaurs descended

ventricle—one of the two lower chambers of the heart that receive blood from the atria and delivery it to the body

vertebrate—an animal with a backbone

warm-blooded—animals who can generate their own body heat and can maintain a relatively constant body temperature

Species Checklist

Each crocodilian species has a scientific name, which is written in Latin. This way, scientists who speak many different languages can refer to each kind of crocodilian in the same way. The scientific name for a species includes the genus, which is capitalized, and the species, which is in lowercase. Both names are written in italics.

Species also have common names, which are used locally. A crocodilian species may have many common names. Some may be in different languages. These names might describe the crocodilian's color, size, shape, or where it lives. Some examples of these, along with the scientific name, appear below.

Family Alligatoridae
Alligator mississippiensis (American alligator, gator)
Alligator sinensis (Chinese alligator, Yangtse alligator, Yow Lung)
Caiman crocodilus (common caiman, spectacled caiman, babilla)
Caiman latirostris (broad-snouted caiman)
Caiman yacare (yacare, Lagarto)
Melanosuchus niger (black caiman, Cocodrilo)
Paleosuchus palpebrosus (Cuvier's dwarf caiman, musky caiman)
Paleosuchus trigonatus (smooth-fronted caiman, Cachirre)

Family Crocodylidae
Crocodylus acutus (American crocodile, caiman de la costa)
Crocodylus cataphractus (slender-snouted crocodile, African gavial)
Crocodylus intermedius (Orinoco crocodile)
Crocodylus johnsoni (Australian freshwater crocodile, freshie, Johnson's crocodile)
Crocodylus mindorensis (Philippine crocodile)
Crocodylus moreletii (Morelet's crocodile, Cocodrilo do pantano)
Crocodylus niloticus (Nile crocodile, Mamba)
Crocodylus novaeguineae (New Guineae crocodile, Pukpuk)
Crocodylus palustris (mugger, marsh crocodile)
Crocodylus porosus (Indo-Pacific crocodile, saltwater/estuarine crocodile, salty)
Crocodylus rhombifer (Cuban crocodile, pearly crocodile)
Crocodylus siamensis (Siamese crocodile, Buaya kodok)

Osteolaemus tetraspis (dwarf crocodile, broad-nosed crocodile)
Tomistoma schlegelii (false gharial, tomistoma, Takong)

Family Gavialidae
Gavialis gangeticus (gharial, gavial)

Further Research

Here are some recommended resources for further research on crocodiles.

Books

Bright, Michael. *Alligators and Crocodiles*. New York: Franklin Watts, 1990.
Covers how and why crocodilians are endangered, and discusses some solutions.

Deeble, Mark and Victoria Stone. *The Crocodile Family Book*. New York: North-South Books, 1994.
The authors relate their experiences photographing crocodiles in Serengeti National Park in Tanzania. Corresponds with the *National Geographic* video listed below.

Dow, Lesley. *Alligators and Crocodiles*. New York: Facts On File, 1990.
Based on the Charles Ross book (see Bibliography), but rewritten for younger readers.

Dudley, Karen. *Alligators and Crocodiles*. Austin: Raintree Steck-Vaughn, 1998.
Fun and informative reading covering a wide range of crocodilian information.

Perry, Phyllis J. *The Crocodilians: Reminders of the Age of the Dinosaurs*. New York: Franklin Watts, 1997.
Portraits of various species of crocodilians with an overview of crocodilian evolution.

Stoops, Erik D. and Debbie Lynne Stone. *Alligators and Crocodiles*. New York: Sterling Publishing Company, 1994.
Question-and-answer format with comprehensive coverage of crocodilians.

Videos

Crocodiles: Here Be Dragons. National Geographic, 1990.
Amazing footage of crocodiles feeding and caring for their hatchlings.

Predators of the Wild: Crocodiles and Alligators. Time-Life, 1994.
> Focuses on the American alligator, the Nile crocodile, and the gharial. Discusses current research and conservation of crocodilians.

Web Sites

http://www.crocodilian.com
> This site includes a species list with details about each crocodilian, a comprehensive section on biology, and a list of many other Internet resources. There is also a communication section where you can hear crocodilians hiss, roar, and squeak!

http://www.discovery.com/stories/nature/crocs/video.html
> Videos of crocodiles in action.

http://www.envirolink.org/oneworld/tales/crocs/intervhtml
> Facts and legends about crocodiles and an interview with an Australian reptile expert named Steve Irwin. His stories are not to be missed.

Bibliography

These are the resources that were most useful in researching this book. Although the publications listed here may include some information that is a bit technical for young readers, they are all worthwhile for those with a strong interest in crocodilians. The video may be difficult to watch because it shows animals suffering from drought, but it will probably change the way you think about animals.

Books

Alderton, David. *Crocodiles and Alligators of the World*. New York: Facts On File, 1991.
Thorough treatment of all aspects of crocodilians. Gives in-depth information about each species. Also includes terrific stories about crocodilian behavior.

Cogger, Dr. Harold G. and Dr. Richard G. Zwiefel. *Reptiles and Amphibians*. New York: Weldon Owen, 1992.
Clearly written overview of reptilian evolution and classification. Good summary of crocodilians.

Minelli, Guiseppi. *Reptiles*. New York: Facts On File, 1987.
Detailed report on the evolution of reptiles.

Ross, Charles. *Crocodiles and Alligators*. New York: Facts On File, 1989.
Almost everything you'd want to know about crocodilians, from their evolution to their present-day status. Also includes amazing photographs.

Rue, Leonard Lee. *Alligators and Crocodiles*. New York: Smithmark, 1994.
Includes great photographs and basic information about crocodilians.

Wilkinson, Richard H. *Symbol and Magic in Egyptian Art*. London: Thames and Hudson, 1994.
Intriguing stories about the ancient Egyptians' relationship with crocodiles and other animals.

Scientific Publications

Ross, James Perron. *Crocodiles: Status Survey and Conservation Action Plan, Second Edition*. Crocodile Specialist Group, 1998.
Comprehensive report accessible via the web site below.

Videos

Last Feast of the Crocodiles. National Geographic, 1995.
Powerful video showing the interactions of crocodiles with other animals who are all struggling to survive during a drought in South Africa.

Web Sites

http://www.flmnh.ufl.edu/natsci/herpetology/crocs.htm
This is the web site of the Crocodile Specialist Group. It includes background information about the CSG, gives access to their newsletter, tells how you can help conserve crocodilians, and has links to many other sites. It also gives access to the latest *Status Survey and Conservation Action Plan*. Besides supplying conservation news, this plan contains comprehensive information about each crocodilian species.

Index

Page numbers for illustrations are in **boldface**.

About the Author

JUDITH JANGO-COHEN grew up in a Boston apartment where the only reptile around was her pet turtle. Always interested in nature, she got a degree in biology and began teaching science to children. During her teaching days, Judith made a trip to the Everglades with her husband Eliot. There, she encountered her first crocodilian. Over the years, she returned to the Everglades many times, bringing along her childen, Jennifer and Steven. Researching and writing about crocodiles for this book was great fun for her—almost as much fun as watching them.